P9-DIB-426

RISE:

The Story of The Egyptian Revolution As Written Shortly Before It Began – 'Al Khan' Comic Strips Published in Egypt in the Lead-Up to the Uprising

Second edition. First edition printed 2011

For more of this author's work please visit www.alkhancomics.com
The author can be reached at tarekshahin@gmail.com

ISBN-13: 978-1461120544

An estimated 850 people were killed in the brutal crackdown against peaceful pro-democracy protests in Egypt between January and February 2011.

This is dedicated to them.

And to Rania Al Malki, editor of The Daily News Egypt, who let me speak my mind long before it was cool to do so.

And to journalist Sarah Sirgany who won plaudits for her valiant coverage of the revolution. She has since forever been my best friend and sounding board.

And to my parents, for listening.

And to Nina, for her patience.

29 April 2010

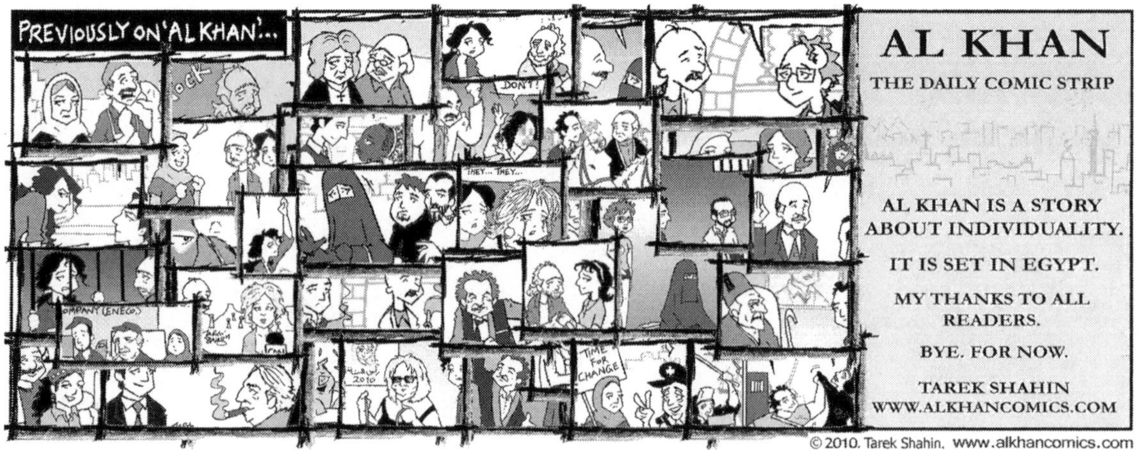
PREVIOUSLY ON 'AL KHAN'...
DON'T!
THEY... THEY...
TIME FOR CHANGE
AL KHAN
THE DAILY COMIC STRIP
AL KHAN IS A STORY ABOUT INDIVIDUALITY.
IT IS SET IN EGYPT.
MY THANKS TO ALL READERS.
BYE. FOR NOW.
TAREK SHAHIN
WWW.ALKHANCOMICS.COM

Epilogue 4 February 2011

I'M STANDING IN TAHRIR SQUARE IN DOWNTOWN CAIRO WHERE MILLIONS OF EGYPTIANS ARE DEMANDING AN END TO AUTHORITARIAN RULE.

AFTER FIGHTING THE PROTESTERS WITH TEAR GAS, LIVE AMMO AND WEAPONIZED CAMELS, THE RULING REGIME IS NOW OFFERING CONCESSIONS BUT TO NO AVAIL.

WE PROMISE CHANGE. BUT WE NEED TIME FOR A SMOOTH TRANSITION!

WHAT PART OF STABILITY ARE YOU AGAINST?!
THE "STAB" PART!

10 February 2011

THE ENTIRE WORLD HAS BEEN CAPTIVATED BY THE IMAGES FROM EGYPT, PERHAPS THE BEST OF WHICH WERE TAKEN BY PHOTOBLOGGER YUNAN SALIB.

HERE TO HELP OUR GLOBAL VIEWERS UNDERSTAND THE SITUATION IS RENOWNED EGYPTIAN SOCIOLOGIST DR. EBAA ANTAR.

DR. EBAA, YOU ARE THE MOST QUALIFIED PERSON HERE TO GIVE INSIGHTS INTO THE EGYPTIAN PSYCHE.

THANK YOU. BECAUSE MY WRITINGS WERE ON EGYPT?
BECAUSE YOUR WRITINGS WERE IN ENGLISH.

11 February 2011

THE FALL OF THE REGIME SEEMS IMMINENT. WHILE WE WAIT WE ASK: HOW DID WE GET HERE?

TAHRIR SQUARE HAS UNITED EGYPTIANS FROM ALL WALKS OF LIFE: RICH AND POOR, MUSLIM AND CHRISTIAN, SECULARIST AND CONSERVATIVE, HUSBAND AND WIFE.

WHY DID THEY COME HERE? WHAT WERE THEY SO ANGRY ABOUT? WHO AT?
Social Justice
عدالة إجتماعية
Freedom
حرية

WHY NOW?
Change
تغيير

The following comic strips were written and published between April 2008 and April 2010.
The three series of "Al Khan" ran every day in The Daily News Egypt, the Egyptian affiliate of the International Herald Tribune.

PART ONE
The Privatization of ENECO

3 May 2008

NADA, I'M RECOMMENDING THAT YOU REPLACE ME AS EDITOR OF 'AL KHAN'.
REPLACE YOU?! MR. ANIS, THAT NEW PUBLISHER, OMAR, IS NOT MAKING YOU LEAVE, IS HE?!
NO, IT'S TIME I STEPPED DOWN. WHEN I FIRST TOOK THIS DESK, EGYPT WAS STILL A KINGDOM! MY HAIR WAS STILL BLACK! CAIRO'S SKY WAS STILL BLUE!!
IT'S JUST THAT YOU NEVER CAME ACROSS AS THE CALIBER OF EGYPTIANS WHO WOULD WILLINGLY STEP DOWN FROM A LEADING POST!
WHAT CALIBER WOULD I NEED TO BE, NADA?!
RECENTLY DECEASED!

7 May 2008

SO I MET OMAR SHUKRI, THE NEW PUBLISHER. HE SEEMS TO BE DECENT, NADA!
PLEASE, YUNAN! HE'S REPULSIVE!!
YOU STILL RESENT THAT HE SAID HE MADE YOU EDITOR AGAINST HIS WILL?!
I RESENT THAT HE THINKS HIS CAPITALIST, NEOLIBERAL VIEWS ARE SUPERIOR TO ALL OTHERS! I MEAN HOW NARROW MINDED AND INTOLERANT CAN ONE BE?!
OH, I HAVE TO STOP HERE. I NEED A NEW JACKET!
MEN FASHION
NO! NOT UNTIL THEY PAY THE TEXTILE WORKERS A HIGHER MINIMUM WAGE!! KEEP MOVING YOU PIG!!

8 May 2008

I SEE YOU'VE SETTLED IN SINCE YOUR RETURN TO CAIRO, OMAR.
قهوة حامد
QAHWA HAMED
YEAH, EXCEPT I DON'T THINK THE STAFF AT THE MAGAZINE LIKE ME, ANWAR!
WELL, OBVIOUSLY, THE FEMALE WORKERS ARE NOT EXPECTED TO TAKE THEIR TERMINATION LIGHTLY AT FIRST! BUT IN TIME...
WHAT ARE YOU TALKING ABOUT?!
YOU DID SEND THE WOMEN HOME WHERE THEY BELONG, DID YOU NOT?!
ANWAR, REMIND ME AGAIN HOW IT IS WE'RE FRIENDS!!

9 May 2008

OMAR!! WHY DID YOU CENSOR MY NEWS STORY?!
AL KHAN

NADA, I NEVER CENSOR! I ONLY TOOK OUT THE WORDS: "VIOLENT RAPE," "WAR MONGERING," AND "ARMAGEDDON"!!

I NOTICED! WHY?!
BECAUSE IT WAS A NEWS STORY ABOUT INDUSTRIAL PRIVATISATION!

YOUR POINT?!

10 May 2008

OMAR, YOU'RE MY BIG BROTHER! EXPLAIN TO ME: WHY DID THE PRICE OF SMOKES OF GO UP?!
WELL, MAGED, WHAT THE PARLIAMENT DID THIS WEEK IS WHAT'S KNOWN AS A 'LIFT OF 'SUBSIDIES.'

YEAH, SO WHY DID THE PRICE OF SMOKES GO UP?
SEE, THE THING ABOUT SUBSIDIES IS THAT THEY'RE EVIL, AND HAVE HISTORICALLY KEPT EGYPTIANS DEVOID OF ANY ENTREPRENEURIAL DRIVE!

LET ME REPHRASE THE QUESTION! CAN I BORROW SOME CASH TO BUY A PACK OF SMOKES?!

13 May 2008

ALO! .. ALO! .... MARWAN! IT'S OMAR SHUKRI FROM CAIRO! WHAT'S HAPPENING IN BEIRUT? HEZBOLLAH DID WHAT?!! ARE YOUR CHILDREN OK? GOOD! AND THE WOMEN?

WAIT! HOW MANY WOMEN DID YOU SAY DIED? AND THE WOMEN INJURED, HOW BADLY DISFIGURED...?

HI, NILE TRAVEL AGENCY? COULD YOU CANCEL MY TICKETS TO BEIRUT AND GET ME A TRIP TO GREECE ON THE SAME DATE?!
YES, ALSO BY THE BEACH!
HELP US..!

14 May 2008

THE JEWS JUST CELEBRATED SIXTY YEARS OF EXISTENCE!
I'M SURE THE JEWISH PEOPLE HAVE BEEN AROUND A LOT LONGER THAN THAT! YOU MEAN ISRAEL!
CHILD-KILLING RAPISTS!
ANWAR, YOU MUST DIFFERENTIATE BETWEEN YOUR DISAPPROVAL OF THE ISRAELI STATE AND THE BLIND CONDEMNATION OF THE ENTIRE JEWISH FAITH!
DON'T GET ME WRONG, OMAR! I THINK ISRAELI PEOPLE ARE WONDERFUL...
GOOD, NOW AT LEAST WE'RE GETTING SOMEWHERE!
...EXCEPT FOR THEIR JEWNESS!

15 May 2008

NADA, WHY DON'T WE HAVE ANY COVERAGE ON ISRAEL'S SIXTIETH ANNIVERSARY?
OF COURSE WE DO! CHECK THE FIRST TWO PAGES OF THIS WEEK'S DRAFT ISSUE!!
ALL I SEE ARE TWO PAGES FILLED WITH RED INK BLOTCHES!
YES, TO SYMBOLIZE BLOOD!
IT DOESN'T SCREAM 'TWO STATE SOLUTION!'
NO SHIT.

19 May 2008

AND, THAT, LADIES AND GENTS, COVERS OUR COUNTRY'S ECONOMIC PLAN. QUESTIONS?
NADA SALEH! 'AL KHAN' MAGAZINE!
WORLD ECONOMIC FORUM
DO YOU BELIEVE THE POLICIES BROUGHT FORWARD TODAY WILL ELEVATE LIVING STANDARDS?
OUR POLICIES AIM TO FOSTER GROWTH AND SECURE SUSTAINABLE RETURNS TO FOREIGN INVESTORS...
...OR, AS WE LIKE TO CALL THEM, THE PEOPLE!

22 May 2008

SO MAGED, I HEARD OUR PRESIDENT WALKED AWAY DURING BUSH'S SPEECH AT THE WORLD ECONOMIC THING!
YEAH! GO EGYPT! MY BROTHER OMAR SAYS IT'S BECAUSE BUSH MADE COMMENTS ABOUT EGYPTIAN HUMAN RICE!
WHO DOES BUSH THINK HE IS?!
YEAH, THESE DAYS MORE AMERICANS ARE DEPRIVED OF THEIR RICE THAN EGYPTIANS!
AND WHO'S TO SAY PEOPLE CAN ONLY HAVE RICE THE AMERICAN WAY?!!
WAIT... COME TO THINK OF IT...
YEAH, MAN... RICE IS RICE!
© 2008. Tarek Shahin. www.alkhancomics.com

23 May 2008

OMAR, IF YOU SUPPORT THE GOVERNMENT PRICE HIKES SO MUCH, WHY DIDN'T YOU GIVE US A 30% WAGE INCREASE LIKE IN THE PUBLIC SECTOR?
WHO ARE YOU?
MY NAME IS ALIA! I'M ONE OF THE REPORTERS HERE AT 'AL KHAN' MAGAZINE!
ALIA, IF I PAY YOU MORE MONEY, WILL YOU SPEND IT ON SCARVES?
BE HONEST!
SOME OF IT, I GUESS. I MEAN, I'M VEILED, SO I NEED TO BUY SCARVES!
HAVE A SEAT, ALIA!
ALIA, YOU'VE BEEN A GREAT ASSET TO 'AL KHAN,' BUT I'M NOT SURE WE HAVE THE FINANCIAL ABILITY TO SUPPORT YOUR LIFESTYLE!
ARE THOSE CUBAN CIGARS?!!
© 2008. Tarek Shahin. www.alkhancomics.com

26 May 2008

LISTEN, YUNAN, WE NEED A PHOTO OF AN EGYPTIAN MIDDLE CLASS FAMILY FOR THIS WEEK'S COVER PAGE!
I'M ON IT!
I'D LIKE THE FATHER TO BE LATE-THIRTIES AND THE MOTHER TO BE VEILED, CHUBBY AND WITH HAZEL EYES, AND WITH FOUR CHILDREN: THREE GIRLS AND ONE BOY.
IT WOULD BE GREAT IF YOU COULD GET THEM TO SIT OUTDOORS WITH A VIEW OF THE CITADEL AGAINST SUNRISE!
YOU THINK YOU CAN MAKE THAT POSSIBLE?
I'M A VETERAN PHOTOGRAPHER, OMAR! I CAN MAKE ANYTHING POSSIBLE!
YOU THINK YOU CAN GET THEM TO SMILE FOR THE CAMERA?!
WITH INFLATION AT 20%? I'M NOT GOD!
© 2008. Tarek Shahin. www.alkhancomics.com

29 May 2008

ANWAR, I CAN'T CONTROL MY BROTHER MAGED'S BEHAVIOR! ...ESPECIALLY NOW AFTER FATHER'S PASSING!
I HAD THAT SAME PROBLEM WITH MY WIFE, AISHA!
THE NEIGHBORS HAD HER BELIEVE SHE HAD THE RIGHT TO DEMAND I BUY US A TELEVISION SET...
...UNTIL I SAT HER DOWN AND GAVE HER 'THE TALK!'
SHE'S NEVER BROUGHT IT UP SINCE!
I FAIL TO SEE THE ANALOGY!
HMMM. YOU'RE RIGHT, OMAR! IT'S NOT LIKE YOU CAN THREATEN MAGED TO MARRY THREE OTHER BROTHERS!
© 2008. Tarek Shahin. www.alkhancomics.com

30 May 2008

THEY EXTENDED THE EMERGENCY LAW FOR TWO MORE YEARS?!
WHAT DID YOU EXPECT, OMAR?!
ALKHAN
I REALLY THINK THE ISLAMIST THREAT IS BEING WRONGLY ESTIMATED!
ABSOLUTELY!
IF YOU THINK ABOUT IT, BETWEEN RISING FOOD PRICES, THE WESTERN INVASION OF THE GULF, AND INCREASING RATES OF FEMALE CIRCUMCISION, THE GOVERNMENT OUGHT TO ADDRESS THE REAL ISSUES INSTEAD OF EXTENDING THE ALMOST 30-YEAR-OLD EMERGENCY LAW, RIGHT?
OMAR? WHERE ARE YOU GOING?!
TWO YEARS MY ASS !!
four more years
© 2008. Tarek Shahin. www.alkhancomics.com

2 June 2008*

DR. AMGAD GAD HAS BEEN APPOINTED MINISTER OF PROSPERITY...
I VOW TO HONOR THE EGYPTIAN CONSTITUTION...
...AND I VOW TO AGGRESSIVELY INSTALL STRUCTURAL REFORM MEASURES...
...WHILE PATRIOTICALLY UPHOLDING THE STATUS QUO!
© 2008. Tarek Shahin. www.alkhancomics.com

Notes by the author:

* "The Ministry of Prosperity" and its head Dr. Gad are both fictional.

3 June 2008*

IN RESPONSE TO THE RECENT UNREST AT 'ENGINEERING NILE EGYPTIAN COMPANY' (ENECO), RECENTLY APPOINTED MINISTER OF PROSPERITY DR. GAD HAS CALLED FOR CALM!
DR. GAD WAS QUOTED AS SAYING, "NO! WE HAVE NO INTENTION WHATSOEVER OF PRIVATISING ENECO!"
YUNAN...
I GUESS I OWE YOU 50 POUNDS!
DAMN, NADA! I REALLY THOUGHT THEY WOULDN'T PRIVATISE THAT ONE!

4 June 2008**

EXCUSE ME, MADAM! COULD YOU GIVE ME SOME CHANGE? ANYTHING TO BUY FOOD!
HERE YOU GO!
THANK YOU, MOST GRACIOUS! ...WHAT THE #@! IS THIS?! I CAN'T EVEN BUY RICE WITH THIS TODAY!
THEN GET A JOB, YOU FILTHY... WAIT! REALLY?! BUT I JUST BOUGHT SOME YESTERDAY AND IT ONLY COST...
YA LAHWY! OH DEAR! I BETTER RUSH TO THE MARKET!
COME BACK IF YOU NEED CASH!

5 June 2008***

I NEED HELP, BIG FALAFEL! WHAT'VE YOU HEARD ABOUT THE GOVERNMENT PRIVATISING ENGINEERING NILE EGYPTIAN COMPANY?
ENECO?! HA HA! NADA, THEY'VE BEEN TALKING ABOUT THAT FOR DECADES! EVEN NASSER HAD SECOND THOUGHTS ABOUT NATIONALISING IT BACK THEN!
WHY?
I DON'T KNOW IF YOU HEARD, BUT NASSER'S WAR IN YEMEN HAD BUDGET PROBLEMS!
I MEANT WHY DO THEY WANT TO PRIVATISE IT NOW?!
NASSER'S WAR IN YEMEN HAD BUDGET PROBLEMS!

Notes by the author:

* Engineering Nile Egyptian Company (ENECO) is a fictional company.

** "Ya Lahwy" is a very Egyptian version of "Oh no!"

*** "Back then" here refers to the 1950s and 1960s.

6 June 2008

OMAR COME! MAGED IS REALLY SCARED ABOUT THE EGYPTIAN HISTORY EXAM HE TOOK THIS MORNING!
I'M GOING TO FAAAIIILLL...

DID YOU GET ONE OF THOSE MULTIPLE CHOICE QUESTIONS WHERE ALL THE ANSWERS SEEM CORRECT?!
YEAH, THESE ARE TERRIBLE!

THE QUESTION ASKED: "IN 1924, THE PEOPLE VOTED FOR: (A) THE WAFD PARTY, (B) THE LIBERAL CONSTITUTIONAL PARTY, OR (C) VOTING WAS POSTPONED."

THAT'S EASY, MAGED! IN 1924, THE...
WHAT THE #@?$ IS "VOTING?!!"

© 2008. Tarek Shahin. www.alkhancomics.com

7 June 2008

AND, THOSE, DR. ANWAR, ARE YOUR RIGHTS AS A HUSBAND.

THANK YOU, YOUR EMINENCE. THAT WAS A FRUITFUL THREE-HOUR SESSION.
WHAT ABOUT MY DUTIES AS A HUSBAND?

SO MORE ON MY RIGHTS NEXT WEEK?
YOU KNOW WHERE TO FIND ME!

© 2008. Tarek Shahin. www.alkhancomics.com

10 June 2008

I HAD A LONG DAY, AISHA. DID YOU MAKE DINNER?
THE KIDS ARE ASLEEP, ANWAR!

WHAT DO YOU HAVE IN MIND?
I WANT TO GET WILD!!

RAaaAARRR

YOU'RE SICK, OMAR! IS THAT REALLY HOW YOU THINK OF ME AND MY WIFE?!!
I TOLD YOU, MAN! THOUGHTS I CAN CONTROL! NIGHTMARES I CAN'T!!

© 2008. Tarek Shahin. www.alkhancomics.com

11 June 2008

OMAR THINKS HE'S ENTITLED TO JUDGE MY BELIEFS!
HE THINKS I AM AN OVERPROTECTIVE CAVEMAN JUST BECAUSE I ASK YOU TO WEAR THE NIQAB WHEN IN PUBLIC!
HAVE WE COME TO AN AGE WHERE A MAN IS RIDICULED FOR HIDING HIS WIFE'S FACE FROM THE HUNGRY EYES OF MEN?!
YOU DON'T THINK I GO TOO FAR, AISHA, DO YOU?
WHATEVER YOU SAY, ANWAR!
© 2008. Tarek Shahin. www.alkhancomics.com

12 June 2008*

قهوة حامد
QAHWA HAMED
HELLO, MY NAME IS NOAH LEVY. I JUST ARRIVED IN CAIRO FROM ENGLAND. I'M A STUDENT OF MIDDLE-EAST STUDIES!
I'M ANWAR. PLEASE SIT. INTERESTING NAME, NOAH!
YES, LIKE THE MAN WHO SAVED HIS FAMILY ON THE ARK!
YOU MEAN EXCEPT FOR THE IDOLATER SON WHO DROWNED!
WELL, YOU SAY TOMATO, I SAY...
YOU'RE PUSHING YOUR LUCK, KHAWAGA!!
© 2008. Tarek Shahin. www.alkhancomics.com

13 June 2008

THANKS FOR THE PRESCRIPTION, DR. ANWAR. I HOPE THE RESIDENTS AT THE BUILDING ARE CHARITABLE TODAY! MEDICINE IS EXPENSIVE!
BY THE WAY, WHERE'S THE NEAREST PHARMACY?
I DON'T KNOW!
I MEAN... WHERE DO YOU BUY YOUR MEDICINE?
I CAN'T AFFORD MEDICINE! I AM A DOCTOR!
Dear readers,
'Al Khan' is committed to make its stories relevant to an international audience.
We therefore apologize to our non-Egyptian readers who have found Dr. Anwar's last comment to be incomprehensible.
To our readers in the West, you are kindly requested to replace Anwar's phrase, "I am a doctor," with "Alimony is a bitch."
Thank you
'Al Khan'
© 2008. Tarek Shahin. www.alkhancomics.com

Notes by the author:

* "Khawaga" is an Arabic term for foreigner.

14 June 2008

PREVIOUSLY ON 'AL KHAN'...
THE MINISTER WAS QUOTED AS SAYING, "NO! WE HAVE NO INTENTION WHATSOEVER OF PRIVATIZING ENECO!
WOW, NADA! I REALLY THOUGHT THEY WOULDN'T PRIVATIZE THAT ONE!
ENECO...
CHIEF RIFAI! IS IT TRUE?! ARE WE LOSING OUR JOBS?!
SON, THERE'S A RECENT ECONOMIC REPORT ON EGYPT. DO YOU KNOW HOW MANY HOURS OF ACTUAL WORK ARE ACCOMPLISHED IN AN 8 HOUR SHIFT IN THE PUBLIC SECTOR?!
TWELVE MINUTES!
REALLY?! 12 MINUTES OF WORK IN 8 HOURS?! YOU MEAN...?
ENGINEERING NILE EGYPTIAN COMPANY (ENECO)
YES! THAT'S UP FROM SIX MINUTES 20 YEARS AGO! WE'VE DOUBLED PRODUCTIVITY WITHOUT ANY PRIVATE SECTOR INVOLVEMENT!
WHY WOULD THEY PRIVATIZE ENECO?!
GOD BLESS YOUR WISDOM, CHIEF RIFAI!

18 June 2008

SALAM ALAIKOM, ABU ALI. THIS IS MY NEW FRIEND, NOAH LEVY FROM ENGLAND. HE'S LOOKING FOR AN APARTMENT.
ANYTHING FOR YOU, DR ANWAR!
I APPRECIATE YOUR HELP, MATE!
SO, ANWAR, CAN YOU ALSO HELP ME SCORE SOME HONEYS?!
MARRIAGE?! OF COURSE! AND DON'T WORRY.. THERE IS A SIZEABLE CHRISTIAN COMMUNITY IN EGYPT!
I'M... NOT CHRISTIAN, MATE!
YOU'RE NOT?! REALLY?! I GUESS I JUST ASSUMED!
SALAM ALAIKOM, YOUR EMINENCE. BROTHER LEVY SEEKS A WIFE!
CAN... CAN I HAVE MY SHOES BACK?!

21 June 2008

NAHED HABIB AND ABLA KAMEL IN EGYPT'S #1 SUMMER COMEDY
CREAMY SEWAGE
WHAT A SHAME!
IT'S A SHAME SEEING A VETERAN ACTRESS LIKE NAHED HABIB STOOP TO THIS LEVEL OF COMMERCIALISM!
YOU KNOW, MAKE A FILM THAT HAS NO STORY AND RELIES ON CRUDE JOKES FOR EASY LAUGHS!!
DON'T YOU AGREE, NADA?
YES!
I MEAN, HAS EGYPTIAN CINEMA LOST ITS INTEGRITY?!
OH! WAIT! ISN'T NAHED HABIB YOUR MOTHER?!
YES. YES, SHE IS!
I'M... I'M SO SORRY, NADA! I DIDN'T MEAN TO...
OMAR, THAT'S THE FIFTH TIME IN THE LAST HOUR THAT YOU'VE ASKED ME IF NAHED HABIB WAS MY MOTHER!

24 June 2008

BASMA, NADA, TO CELEBRATE THE SUCCESS OF MY NEW MOVIE, I'M BUYING EACH OF YOU A PAIR OF PRADA SHOES!
MOTHER, I APPRECIATE THE GESTURE BUT I CAN'T ACCEPT YOUR PRESENTS!
COME ON, NADA! DO YOU STILL BLAME ME FOR YOUR FATHER LEAVING? HE LEFT BECAUSE HE WAS NOT AS SUCCESSFUL A WRITER AS I WAS AN ACTRESS!
IN OTHER WORDS, HE WASN'T A SELLOUT!
ENOUGH!!!
ENOUGH WITH THIS PROLONGED, DESTRUCTIVE DOMESTIC ARGUMENT!! THERE IS A GREATER ISSUE STILL UNRESOLVED!!!
NOW, CAN IT BE ASSUMED THAT THE PAIR OF SHOES NADA IS NOT TAKING IS NOW...
WE'RE AWARE IT'S WEDDING SEASON IN CAIRO, BASMA! YOU HAVE MY BLESSING!
© 2008. Tarek Shahin. www.alkhancomics.com

26 June 2008

BABA, COULD I HAVE SOME MONEY TO GO WATCH "CREAMY SEWAGE" AT THE CINEMA?
IS THIS MOVIE FOR CHILDREN?
I DON'T KNOW!
WELL, SON, HOW ABOUT IF BABA ANWAR GIVES YOU MONEY INSTEAD TO BUY A BOOK ABOUT THE PAIN THAT AWAITS SINNERS IN HELL?
IS THAT FOR CHILDREN?!
© 2008. Tarek Shahin. www.alkhancomics.com

1 July 2008

OMAR, HOW CAN YOU ARGUE THAT PRIVATIZING ENECO IS A GOOD THING?!
HOW CAN YOU ARGUE THAT IT'S NOT, NADA?!
SELLING THE COMPANY TO THE PRIVATE SECTOR WILL RESULT IN MASSIVE LAYOFFS!
GREATER EFFICIENCY!
ABNORMAL PROFITS!
HIGHER TAX REVENUE!
UNEVEN DISTRIBUTION OF INCOME!
UNEVEN DISTRIBUTION OF INCOME!
© 2008. Tarek Shahin. www.alkhancomics.com

3 July 2008

THERE'S NO CONVINCING YOU, OMAR! YOU HAVE NO REGARD FOR EQUALITY! YOU THINK SELLING ENECO IS GOOD BECAUSE IT RAISES THE GROSS DOMESTIC PRODUCT! WELL, THERE ARE MORE IMPORTANT THINGS THAN A HIGHER GDP!
LIKE WHAT?!

LIKE A HIGHER GDP PER CAPITA! SO THAT YOU, ME AND THAT FAMILY OVER THERE CAN ALL LIVE PROSPEROUS!
NADA, LET ME EXPLAIN TO YOU WHY EQUALITY IS UNFAIR!

GDP....

....PER CAPITA
?

© 2008. Tarek Shahin. www.alkhancomics.com

4 July 2008

AL KHAN

YUNAN, HAVE YOU SEEN NADA OR OMAR? I NEED SOMEONE TO SIGN OFF ON THE DRAFT BEFORE IT GOES TO THE PRINTERS!

OMAR! THE SALE OF ENECO WILL HAVE DIRE SOCIAL EFFECTS!!
YES, NADA, IF BY 'DIRE' YOU MEAN 'MUCH NEEDED'!!!

I HATE IT WHEN MOM AND DAD FIGHT!

© 2008. Tarek Shahin. www.alkhancomics.com

5 July 2008

LONDON: 8 MONTHS AGO...
OMAR, THE BOSSES UPSTAIRS ARE ANGRY ABOUT THE NEGATIVE REPORT YOU WROTE ON THE CLIENTS!
THEY HAVE NEGATIVE CASH FLOW! I ONLY WROTE THE TRUTH!

CAIRO: TODAY
I KNOW WHY YOU WON'T PUBLISH MY STORY, OMAR! YOU LACK INTEGRITY!
YOUR PROBLEM, NADA, IS THAT YOU THINK YOU HAVE A MONOPOLY ON ETHICS!

YOU'RE RISKING YOUR CAREER, MATE! ARE YOU AWARE OF LONDON BONUSES?!
ARE THEY AWARE OF MY MIDDLE FINGER?!

HA! SAID THE FORMER INVESTMENT BANKER TO THE TRUTH-SEEKING JOURNALIST!

© 2008. Tarek Shahin. www.alkhancomics.com

7 July 2008

I HOPE I'M DOING A GOOD JOB RUNNING 'AL KHAN', GRANDFATHER. EVERY BODY THERE MISSES YOUR DAYS AS THE PUBLISHER.
ZZZ... HUH? WHAT?! DID THE MILITARY INVADE THE PALACE YET?!
GRANDFATHER, IT'S 2008! THE 'FREE OFFICERS' STAGED THE COUP IN 1952!!
DID THEY INVADE THE PALACE YET?!
FOCUS, GRANDFATHER! THE MILITARY MARCHED IN MANY DECADES AGO! IT'S ANCIENT HISTORY!!
AH, THAT'S RIGHT! THAT'S RIGHT!
ARE THEY GONE NOW?
GRANDFATHER, IT'S STILL 2008!
NOT YET!

9 July 2008

I CAN'T COPE, BABA! SINCE GRANDFATHER'S RETIREMENT, THE EDITORS OF 'AL KHAN' STILL HAVEN'T ACCEPTED ME AS THE NEW PUBLISHER.
MAGED CAN'T ACCEPT ME AS AN OLDER BROTHER. AND MAMA, LIKE ME, CAN'T ACCEPT THE FACT THAT YOU'RE NO LONGER WITH US.
I GUESS WHAT I'M SAYING IS THAT YOUR PASSING HAS LEFT ME WITH A LOT OF QUESTIONS.
CHIEF AMONG THEM: WHICH PART IS THE CARBURETOR?!
AUTO BILL

10 July 2008

MONA, I KNOW OMAR IS YOUR SON BUT HE'S ALSO MY NEPHEW. WE NEED TO FIND HIM A BRIDE!
SOHA, I THINK OMAR IS OLD ENOUGH TO MAKE HIS OWN DECISIONS!
HE'S PUSHING 30, MONA! HE GOT SO CONSUMED IN HIS CAREER HE LOST SIGHT OF HIS NEEDS!
HE NEEDS TO START A FAMILY! BESIDES, A GOOD BOY LIKE OMAR NEEDS TO GET MARRIED BEFORE HE PLUNGES INTO THE ABYSS OF PREMARITAL SIN!
ACTUALLY...
OMAR AND I AGREE!

12 July 2008

WHERE ARE YOU GOING, OMAR? YOU FINISHED YOUR SHISHA ALREADY?
I'M MEETING YUNAN, MY COLLEAGUE. WE'RE WATCHING THAT NEW FILM, "HASSAN AND MORQOS"
HAVEN'T HEARD OF IT. CAN I COME TOO?
IT STARS ADEL IMAM AND OMAR SHARIF. BUT I DON'T THINK IT'S YOUR KIND OF MOVIE, ANWAR!
WHY NOT?!
WELL... IT'S ABOUT A COPT AND A MUSLIM AND THE HARMONY AMONG EGYPTIANS OF DIFFERENT FAITHS!
OH, COME ON, PLEASE LET ME COME! YOU KNOW HOW MUCH I ENJOY FICTION!
© 2008. Tarek Shahin. www.alkhancomics.com

15 July 2008*

DR. ATEF SALIB PHARMACY
صيدلية
د. عاطف صليب
YUNAN, YOU'RE TELLING ME THIS IS YOUR FATHER'S PHARMACY?!
WHY ARE YOU SO SURPRISED, OMAR?
HE'S "SALIB." I THOUGHT YOUR LAST NAME WAS "SALIBA." COME TO THINK OF IT, I ALWAYS DID THINK "SALIBA" SOUNDED A BIT LEVANTINE!
IT'S NOT LIKE YOU'LL GET MORE WORK IF YOU USE A LEBANESE NAME!
THE 90s, MAN!
14 YEARS AGO...
HELLO, I'M HERE TO PRESENT MY PORTFOLIO TO THE ART DIRECTOR. MY NAME IS YUNAN SALIB.
JUST LEAVE IT WITH THIS PILE AND LEAVE!
SPORTS
...BA.
SEND HIM IN IMMEDIATELY!!
WELCOME TO EGYPT!
© 2008. Tarek Shahin. www.alkhancomics.com

16 July 2008

YUNAN, SON, WE BELIEVE THERE IS NOW A CHANCE FOR YOU TO FINALLY GET MARRIED!
I READ IN THE PAPER THEY MAY LOWER THE ACCEPTANCE GRADE AT CAIRO'S FACULTY OF MEDICINE! WHICH MEANS YOU HAVE A SHOT!
BABA, YOU'RE A PHARMACIST AND THAT MAKES YOU PROUD AND I'M A PHOTOGRAPHER AND THAT MAKES ME PROUD!
I'M NOT GOING TO MEDICAL SCHOOL!!
BESIDES, I'M OVER 40 NOW! BY THE TIME I FINISH SEVEN YEARS OF MEDICAL SCHOOL PLUS ANOTHER TEN YEARS OF POST GRADUATE STUDIES I'LL BE ALMOST 60 BEFORE PEOPLE CALL ME DR. YUNAN!
WE LOOK FORWARD TO IT!
YOUR MOTHER AND I JOINED A GYM!
© 2008. Tarek Shahin. www.alkhancomics.com

Notes by the author:

* Cable TV introduced Al Jazeera News and Lebanese hotties to the Egyptian household.

22 July 2008

PREVIOUSLY ON 'AL KHAN'...
DR. AMGAD GAD HAS BEEN APPOINTED MINISTER OF PROSPERITY
I VOW TO INSTALL REFORMS AND UPHOLD THE STATUS QUO...

YOUR EXCELLENCY!! EMERGENCY!! PEOPLE HAVE BEEN ALERTED TO THE PLAN TO PRIVATIZE ENGINEERING NILE EGYPTIAN COMPANY (ENECO)!!

IMPOSSIBLE! ONLY THREE PEOPLE IN THE WHOLE COUNTRY KNOW ABOUT IT!!
WELL, THE INDEPENDENT NEWS MAGAZINE 'AL KHAN' WROTE A STORY!

OH NO! NOW IT'LL BE KNOWN TO THIRTEEN, MAYBE EVEN FOURTEEN PEOPLE!!

24 July 2008

I'M GLAD WE PUT OUR DIFFERENCES ASIDE AND PUBLISHED THE ENECO STORY, NADA. BY THE WAY, WHERE WAS EVERYONE YESTERDAY?
YESTERDAY WAS A NATIONAL HOLIDAY, OMAR!! 23 JULY, TO CELEBRATE THE 1952 REVOLUTION!
AL KHAN ENECO TO BE SOLD

OH, YOU MEAN THE MILITARY COUP!
REVOLUTION!!

MILITARY COUP!!
REVOLUTION!!

MILITARY COUP!!!
REVOLUTION!!!
AL KHAN
SIR, WE'VE LOCATED THE DISSIDENT JOURNALISTS WHO BROKE THE ENECO STORY!
THEY SEEM TO BE PLANNING SOMETHING!

26 July 2008

IN RESPONSE TO WHAT'S BEEN PUBLISHED IN CERTAIN PRINTED MEDIA; YES, THE EGYPTIAN GOVERNMENT PLANS TO PRIVATIZE ENGINEERING NILE EGYPTIAN COMPANY (ENECO).

SOMEWHERE IN CAIRO, EGYPT
WHAT?! THEY'RE SEEKING A STRATEGIC INVESTOR TO ACQUIRE ENECO?
CALL IN MY ANALYSTS!!

ELSEWHERE IN CAIRO, EGYPT
WHAT?! THE GOVERNMENT IS SELLING ENECO?
DROP EVERYTHING! FAMILY MEETING!!

SOMEWHERE IN DOHA, QATAR
WHAT?! EGYPT IS SELLING SOMETHING?!
WHY CAN I NEVER FIND CHANGE WHEN I NEED IT?!

28 July 2008

CAIRO: 1952
MR. SHARIF! IN THE NAME OF THE REVOLUTION, WE HEREBY SEIZE YOUR PROPERTY!
THAT'S MR. SHARIF 'BEY' TO YOU, YOU PEASANT THUGS!!
1962
MAMA, WHAT'S WRONG WITH PAPA? IS HE ILL?
ASHRAF, YOUR FATHER ISN'T USED TO MANUAL LABOR! BUT IF WORKING FOR ENGINEERING NILE EGYPTIAN COMPANY WILL PUT FOOD ON THE TABLE THEN THAT'S WHAT HE NEEDS TO DO!
1976
SORRY TO HEAR ABOUT YOUR FATHER, ASHRAF!
ASHRAF?
I CALL IT 'INFITAH,' AN OPEN DOOR POLICY DURING WHICH, AS YOUR PRESIDENT, I PROMISE THOSE WITH WITS AND A PAIR OF NUTS UNLIMITED WEALTH...
PRESENT DAY
WHAT?! THEY'RE SEEKING A STRATEGIC INVESTOR TO ACQUIRE ENGINEERING NILE EGYPTIAN COMPANY?!
THAT BITCH IS MINE!!

29 July 2008

CAIRO: 1967
FOLLA! THE QUE AT THE KOSHARI STAND IS HUGE!
I GUESS PEOPLE EAT MORE WHEN THEY'RE IN A BAD MOOD! THANK NASSER FOR LOSING THE WAR!
1981
BUSINESS IS SLOW AT THE KOSHARI STAND, MAMA FOLLA!
SHIT! I GUESS PEOPLE HAVE BEEN IN GOOD SPIRITS!!
OH NO! SADAT'S BEEN SHOT!!
1999
مجموعة شركات
الحاجة فلة وأولادها
HAJJA FOLLA & SONS
GROUP OF COMPANIES
IN EGYPT SINCE 1967
KOSHARI
CURRENCY EXCHANGE
TRANSLATION SERVICES
SOFTWARE PROGRAMMING
WASABI IMPORTS
PRESENT DAY
WHAT?! THE GOVERMENT IS SELLING THE INDUSTRIAL ASSETS OF ENECO?!
FAMILY MEETING! IT'S TIME WE GOT INTO REAL ESTATE!!

30 July 2008*

EARTH: 180 MILLION YEARS AGO
HMMM, I WONDER WHAT HAPPENS TO US WHEN WE DIE AND GET BURIED UNDER LAYERS AND LAYERS OF MUD!
ARABIAN GULF DESERT: 1938
HOLY COW! JACKSON! PETE! GUYS, YOU GOTTA COME SEE THIS! I THINK WE JUST FOUND OIL UNDERNEATH 'EM TOWEL HEADS!
DOHA, QATAR: 2005
SHEIKH AZIZ! THE COUNTRY'S BUDGET SURPLUS HAS JUMPED 1600% EVER SINCE OIL INCREASED FROM 35 DOLLARS TO 39 DOLLARS PER BARREL!
PRESENT DAY
BREAKING NEWS: OIL AT $139 PER BARREL
WHAT'S ENECO? EGYPT IS SELLING SOMETHING?!
WHY CAN I NEVER FIND CHANGE WHEN I NEED IT?!

Notes by the author:

* Qatar is a gas-rich country but oil would have been a better recognized proxy.

1 August 2008

THANK YOU FOR TAKING ME TO THE FUNERAL, NADA.
I KNOW HOW MUCH YOUSSEF CHAHINE MEANT TO YOU, MOTHER.
DID I EVER TELL YOU JOE GAVE ME MY FIRST ON-SCREEN ROLE?
YES. YOU TOLD US MANY TIMES BEFORE!
HE WAS SHOOTING THE BATTLE SCENE IN "SALADIN THE VICTORIOUS"...
MOTHER! THERE ARE PLENTY OF WAYS YOU CAN REMIND US THAT YOU USED TO HAVE A SLIMMER FIGURE...
...AND HE RAN OUT OF SPEARS!
...WITHOUT EXAGGERATING!
© 2008. Tarek Shahin. www.alkhancomics.com

4 August 2008

THIS TRAFFIC ISN'T MOVING!! GRRR! SOMETIMES THIS CITY DRIVES ME CRAZY!!
OMAR! YOU CAN'T BEEP YOUR HORN! NEW TRAFFIC LAW TAKES EFFECT IN AUGUST!
BEEP BEEP!
THERE IS A DONKEY CART BLOCKING THE ROAD, ANWAR! WHAT AM I SUPPOSED TO DO? REASON WITH IT?!
WOULD YOU RATHER GO TO PRISON?!
HEY! DONKEY! YOU ARE BLOCKING THE ROAD AND, QUITE FRANKLY, YOU ARE A HINDRANCE TO OUR PROGRESS AS A SOCIETY!!
WOW!! YOU REALLY HIT A NERVE! I NEVER KNEW DONKEYS HAD FEELINGS!
I NEVER KNEW THEY HAD FINGERS!!
© 2008. Tarek Shahin. www.alkhancomics.com

6 August 2008

THIS IS CRAZY, BROTHER LEVY! 180 MEMBERS OF FATAH ESCAPED GAZA INTO ISRAEL?!
ISRAEL ALLOWS GAZANS ENTRY
HAMAS IS SCARING FATAH SO THEY ASK THE JEWS TO PROTECT THEM?!
NOTHING MAKES SENSE ANY MORE!! DO YOU UNDERSTAND THIS?!!
TELL ME, DOES ANY OF THIS MAKE SENSE?!
THAT THEY'D FIND SANCTUARY IN THE ONLY DEMOCRATIC COUNTRY IN THE MIDDLE EAST?
UNFATHOMABLE!
© 2008. Tarek Shahin. www.alkhancomics.com

9 August 2008

COME ON, OMAR! THERE MUST BE SOME GIRL ON THIS BEACH YOU FIND ATTRACTIVE! WHAT IS IT ABOUT JANE THAT MAKES HER SO UNFORGETTABLE!
I DON'T KNOW, MAGED! SOMEHOW, I STILL HAVE FEELINGS FOR JANE! BESIDES, SHE'S MY LAST LINK TO MY LIFE IN...
... LONDON.
... LONDON.
IT'S FUNNY, YOU AND I SAID THE SAME WORD! I WAS TALKING ABOUT MY EX... ABOUT SOMEONE I KNEW...
WE WERE DISCUSSING CITIES THAT BEST MATCH OUR HAIR COLOR!
I'M OMAR!
I'M LEILA!
AND BY THE WAY, WE'VE NARROWED IT DOWN TO LONDON AND CAIRO! WHAT DO YOU THINK?
© 2008. Tarek Shahin.

12 August 2008

YOU MUST UNDERSTAND THAT BY ACQUIRING YOUR ASSETS, WE ARE NOT UNDERMINING YOUR CULTURE, NEITHER ARE WE TAKING YOUR HARD WORK FOR GRANTED...
... BUT THERE IS A NEWER NEW WORLD ORDER! HIGHER GAS PRICES HAVE SIMULTANEOUSLY BROUGHT YOUR ECONOMY TO A RECESSION AND DRIVEN OUR WEALTH THROUGH THE ROOF!
WHEN ABU DHABI BOUGHT YOUR CHRYSLER BUILDING LAST MONTH, THEY DID NOT MAKE ANY CHANGES TO IT, DESPITE THE MISGUIDED FEARS OF MANY NEW YORKERS!
AND YOU TOO MUST TRUST THAT I COME FROM QATAR WITH NO INTENTION OF CHANGING YOUR BUSINESS MODEL ONCE I ACQUIRE YOUR EMPIRE...
ALTHOUGH I MIGHT BUILD A MOSQUE ON YOUR LAWN, IN CASE YOU WISH TO CONVERT!
© 2008. Tarek Shahin.
'Uncle Scrooge' is the property of Disney

14 August 2008

SO WHO ARE THE THREE SUITORS WHO ARE BIDDING FOR ENECO?
THERE'S ASHRAF SHARIF. HE'S OLD MONEY AND NEW MONEY! LOOK INTO HIS QUESTIONABLE BUSINESS PRACTICES...
THERE'S HAJJA FOLLA. SHE'S A MODERN EGYPTIAN FAIRYTALE, NADA! STARTED OUT WITH A KOSHARI STAND AND CLIMBED TO THE TOP WITH A DIVERSIFIED BUSINESS EMPIRE!
SHE'S CLEAN ENOUGH, BUT SHE MAY BE EYEING ENECO FOR THE WRONG REASONS...
... AND THEN THERE'S SHEIKH AZIZ BIN AZIZI.
HE'S FLYING IN FROM QATAR.
HE'S ... WELL...
HE'S THE GULFIE!
BIG FALAFEL! I DON'T THINK 'GULFIE' IS AN APPROPRIATE TERM!
I DON'T THINK 'SUITORS' IS AN APPROPRIATE TERM! WHY IS EGYPT ALWAYS THE WOMAN?!
© 2008. Tarek Shahin. www.alkhancomics.com

18 August 2008

OMAR... I THINK YOU'RE AN AMAZING MAN, AND I'M LUCKY TO BE...
SAY NO MORE, LEILA! I'M THE LUCKY ONE!

WHEN I CAME BACK TO CAIRO, I NEVER IMAGINED I'D FIND SOMEONE LIKE YOU.

...SOMEONE WHO'S SO BEAUTIFUL...

...SOMEONE WHO'S SO WORTHY... ...OF ME!

20 August 2008

LEILA, WE'VE BEEN SEEING EACH OTHER FOR TWO WEEKS NOW... I NEED TO BE HONEST ABOUT MY FEELINGS...

...THE TRUTH IS...

...I FEEL...

...TOO OLD TO BE POKED!
OH, OMAR, I THOUGHT FACEBOOK WOULD BRING US CLOSER!

27 August 2008

ANWAR, IS IT WRONG FOR ME TO PURSUE A PHYSICAL RELATION WITH LEILA THIS CLOSE TO RAMADAN?
OMAR! IT'S WRONG TO ENGAGE IN PREMARITAL RELATIONS AT ALL!!

BESIDES, DON'T JUST ASSUME THAT GIRLS HERE ARE AS CASUAL ABOUT THAT KIND OF THING AS THE GIRLS YOU USED TO KNOW ABROAD!
HEY, I'M JUST RESPONDING TO HER SIGNALS! SHE SAID SHE WANTED TO "MOVE TO THE NEXT STEP!"
IN EGYPT THAT MEANS MARRIAGE!!

WHAT? STILL?!
OH NO! PLEASE TELL ME THOSE WERE RINGS YOU JUST BOUGHT FROM THE PHARMACY!!

30 August 2008

HELLO. MY CHILDREN ARE NOT ALLOWED TO GO TO SCHOOL BECAUSE I AM OF BAHAI FAITH!
MAN! I TOLD NADA TO FIRE THAT CARTOONIST!
FIRST HE RIDICULES CONSERVATIVE MUSLIMS, THEN HE MAKES LIGHT OF COPTIC FAMILY VALUES, THEN HE INTRODUCES A JEWISH CHARACTER, AND NOW THIS?!! THE READERS OF 'AL KHAN' ARE NOT READY FOR A BAHAI CHARACTER!!
UNDERSTOOD, BUT FROM WHAT I HEAR, HE DOESN'T LIKE TO BE TOLD WHAT TO WRITE!
WELL, HE MUST RESPECT THE FEELINGS OF THE EGYPTIAN COMMUNITY! HE CAN'T JUST WRITE ANY CHARACTER AS HE PLEASES!
HELLO. I'M GAY!
HELLO. I THINK GOHARY WAS A BETTER COACH THAN SHEHATA!
HELLO. I WALK INTO A ROOM WITH MY LEFT FOOT FIRST!
FINE! YOU MADE YOUR POINT!

1 September 2008

ALL SET, HAJJA FOLLA! YOUR ANNUAL RAMADAN CHARITY EATERY IS READY! YOU'LL BE FEEDING 1,000 PEOPLE AT TODAY'S IFTAR!
مائدة الرحمن
ADD MORE TABLES, TO ACCOMODATE 500 MORE PEOPLE!
FEELING EXTRA CHARITABLE THIS YEAR, HAJJA?
I WANT TO WIN THE BID FOR ENECO WHEN THE GOVERNMENT AUCTIONS THE COMPANY! I NEED GOD'S BLESSING!
GOD'S BLESSING. GOT YOU. BOY!! ADD MORE TABLES!!
I REALLY DON'T WANT TO TAKE GOD'S BLESSING FOR GRANTED THIS YEAR!
AND WASH THE VEGETABLES!!

2 September 2008

HOW COME NONE OF YOU SHOWED UP FOR THE MORNING MEETING?!
IT'S RAMADAN, OMAR! FASTING IS HARD!
ALSO, FASTING REQUIRES BOTH A PHYSICAL AND A SPIRITUAL COMMITMENT! AND ALTHOUGH ALLAH FORBIDS USING RAM-ADAN AS AN EXCUSE FOR SLOPPY WORK, IT IS ALSO YOUR DUTY AS THE BOSS TO MAKE AN ALLOWANCE FOR FASTING AND PRAYER DURING THIS HOLY MONTH!
THAT'S NOT AN EXCUS... WAIT!!! YUNAN, YOU'RE COPTIC!! WHY ARE YOU FASTING?!!
I'M NOT.
AL KHAN
BUT ALIA'S MY RIDE!
AL KHAN

8 September 2008

DR. ANWAR! HELP US! MY BROTHER IS STILL TRAPPED UNDER THE RUBBLE!
I'M TRYING! I'M TRYING!
DR. ANWAR!
I'M STANDING AT THE SITE OF THE DEADLY ROCKSLIDE THAT KILLED DOZENS IN A SHANTYTOWN IN CAIRO!
MANY ARE VOLUNTEERING TO HELP SURVIVORS, INCLUDING LOCAL DOCTORS!
HELLO THERE! DO YOU THINK OUR VIEWERS IN THE WEST WILL JUDGE THE EGYPTIAN GOVERNMENT NEGATIVELY AFTER THIS INCIDENT?
WILL IT AFFECT FOREIGN AID? SHOULD IRAN BE BOMBED?
WHAT'S YOUR BLOOD TYPE?!!
UNFORTUNATELY, THE EGYPTIAN EVASIVENESS AND LACK OF FOCUS PREVAILS!
BACK TO YOU!
CNN

9 September 2008

THE PROUD MAADI SISTERHOOD (PMS) IS HONORED TO HOST PROMINENT BUSINESSMAN ASHRAF SHARIF AT OUR ANNUAL IFTAR!
AND NOW FOR QUESTIONS...
NADA SALEH, 'AL KHAN.'
MR. SHARIF, THERE SEEMS TO BE A GAP BETWEEN THE TIME YOUR FAMILY LOST THEIR WEALTH IN THE 1950s AND YOUR SUDDEN FORTUNE IN THE LATE 1970s!
HOW DARE YOU!! I BUILT MY EMPIRE BRICK BY BRICK, STARTING WITH A LEGITIMATE TRADE AGENCY!
HARD WORKING MEN LIKE ME MADE SADAT'S 'OPEN DOOR' POLICY A SUCCESS!!
HOW MUCH LONGER DO YOU THINK YOU CAN LIE TO THE PEOPLE?!
THERE'S STILL TWO MINUTES TO IFTAR!

10 September 2008

OMAR, I THINK WE SHOULD FEATURE A PROFILE OF ASHRAF SHARIF!
LET ME GUESS, HE'S RICH, WHICH MAKES HIM A SUSPECT IN NADA'S BIG CONSPIRACY THEORY!
I KNOW A PERSON IS INNOCENT UNTIL PROVEN GUILTY BUT IT'S STILL OUR DUTY AS JOURNALISTS TO EXPOSE THE FACTS TO THE READERS AND LET THEM BE THE JUDGE!
SHUT UP, OMAR!!!
WHAT?!! EVERY NOW AND THEN YOU DO MAKE A VALID POINT!!

12 September 2008

THE BEAUTIFUL HOSTAGE
STARRING NAHED HABIB AND MOHAMED ZAZA
EPISODE 12
WHERE AM I?
I ASKED FOR YOUR DAUGHTER'S HAND IN MARRIAGE AND YOU THREW ME OUT !!
IS IT BECAUSE I AM POOR? WHAT IS IT THAT YOU THINK I CAN'T PROVIDE YOUR DAUGHTER ?!
MY CONSENT! AND THIS ISN'T HELPING!
WELL THEN, IT SEEMS I HAVE ONLY ONE CHOICE.... WHICH I WILL DECIDE AFTER THE COOKING OIL COMMERCIALS!
© 2008. Tarek Shahin. www.alkhancomics.com

15 September 2008

OMAR, I JUST SPOKE TO MAGED. YOU DIDN'T TELL ME YOU WERE SEEING THIS NEW GIRL, LEILA!!
WHY CAN'T MAGED KEEP HIS MOUTH SHUT?!
MAMA, I WAS WAITING TO TELL YOU AFTER RAMADAN! I DIDN'T WANT YOU TO COMMIT TO INVITING LEILA OVER FOR SOME BIG IFTAR!
NOT AT ALL! I'D BE HAPPY TO INVITE LEILA AND HER PARENTS OVER FOR IFTAR THIS WEEK!
HER PARENTS?!
MAGED, WHAT EXACTLY DID YOU TELL MAMA?!
NOTHING!! I ONLY SAID YOU WERE SEEING THIS GIRL! SHE DIDN'T ASK ME ABOUT YOUR INTENTIONS!
© 2008. Tarek Shahin. www.alkhancomics.com

19 September 2008*

KNOCK KNOCK
YES?
ARE YOU FORSOOTHSAYER. BLOGSPOT.COM ?
MY NAME IS YUNAN SALIB. I READ YOUR BLOG POST ABOUT HOW TO EXPERIENCE THE MONTH OF RAMADAN! IT'S SUCH A REVELATION! THANK YOU FOR PROVIDING SO MANY ANSWERS!
SO I UNDERSTAND YOU HAVE ACCESS TO BOOZE!
COME IN! CAN I CALL YOU YUNINGS?
© 2008. Tarek Shahin. www.alkhancomics.com

Notes by the author:

* The "ings" in "Yunings" was an inside joke with the blogger who is a real person.

26 September 2008

NADA, COME WATCH MOTHER'S SHOW WITH ME!
NOT NOW, BASMA! I'M WORKING!

OK, I NEED TO CONFIRM MY DOUBTS ABOUT MR. SHARIF'S BUSINESS! I NEED EVIDENCE.

I NEED TO CONCENTRATE. I NEED TO COMPILE MY SOURCES. I NEED TO FOCUS.

I NEED...
YOU NEED A MAN!

27 September 2008

BROTHERS AND SISTERS, THE LAST FEW YEARS HAVE SEEN OUR NATION DEVOURED BY FOREIGNERS AND BETRAYED BY THE LOCAL ELITE WHO HAVE ENSLAVED OUR WORKING CLASS!

NATIONALIZING WILL RESTORE WHAT IS LEFT OF THE DIGNITY OF OUR PEOPLE AND WILL FINALLY ALLOW US TO BUILD AN ECONOMY BASED ON EQUALITY

SO THAT WE MAY RISE AGAIN AS A NATION! WHO'S WITH ME?!!
WHAT'S THAT NOISE, NADA? AN OLD RECORDING OF COLONEL NASSER GIVING HIS VISION FOR 1953?

NO, OMAR, IT'S ACTUALLY A LIVE FEED FROM THE UNITED STATES CONGRESS, DEBATING THEIR VISION FOR 2009!

7 October 2008

SO, ASHRAF, I HEARD YOU LOST A FORTUNE ON THOSE U.S. STOCKS.
THANK YOU FOR ASKING, YOUR EXCELLENCY. BUT DON'T WORRY ABOUT ME! I ALWAYS LAND ON MY FEET!

HAVING SAID THAT, I WAS HOPING YOU'D ALTER THE PROCESS OF AUCTIONING 'ENGINEERING NILE EGYPTIAN COMPANY' SO AS TO MAKE IT... LESS COMPETITIVE!
ASHRAF, MY MINISTRY IS PART OF A REFORM CABINET! THE CORRUPT WAYS OF THE PAST ARE OVER!

COME ON, AMGAD! FOR OLD TIMES' SAKE! WE WENT TO SCHOOL TOGETHER AS KIDS!
YES, AND I REMEMBER YOU USED TO STEAL FROM ME ALL THE TIME!

YOU WERE COOL BACK THEN! WHAT CHANGED?!
EGYPT IS NOT A PENCIL SHARPENER!

8 October 2008

RAMADAN IS FINALLY OVER, YUNAN! I CAN NOW RESUME MY MOVES ON LEILA!
I DIDN'T THINK RAMADAN WAS THE ONLY OBSTACLE, OMAR!
I'M NOT FOLLOWING.
WELL, WHAT YOU HAVE IN MIND WITH THIS GIRL IS A YEAR-ROUND SIN!
NO WONDER THIS COUNTRY IS ABOUT TO EXPLODE! COME ON YUNAN, YOU'RE LIKE 45 YEARS OLD! YOU'RE TELLING ME YOU NEVER ONCE...?
I NEVER GOT MARRIED, OMAR. SO, NO! I DON'T WANT TO GO TO HELL WHEN I DIE!
AM I WRONG? CAN YOU THINK OF MANY THINGS WORSE THAN BEING IN HELL?!
NOT MANY. JUST ONE.
© 2008. Tarek Shahin. www.alkhancomics.com

11 October 2008

PREVIOUSLY ON 'AL KHAN'...
OMAR, IT'S OUR DUTY AS JOURNALISTS TO EXPOSE ASHRAF SHARIF AS CORRUPT BEFORE HE BIDS FOR ENECO!
EASY, NADA! I DON'T DISAGREE! OCCASIONALLY YOU DO MAKE A VALID POINT! LET'S GET THIS GUY!
WOW, LEILA! YOU HAVE AN AMAZING VILLA! THANKS FOR INVITING ME!
I'M SO EXCITED THAT YOU'LL FINALLY GET TO MEET MY FATHER! THERE HE IS... HI DADDY!!
YOU MUST BE OMAR. WELCOME!
YOU HAVE GOT TO BE KIDDING!
HELLO, OMAR. I'M ASHRAF SHARIF.
I... I KNOW WHO YOU ARE!
TO BE CONTINUED....
© 2008. Tarek Shahin. www.alkhancomics.com

13 October 2008

SO, OMAR, LEILA TELLS ME YOU WORK FOR A MAGAZINE.
ACTUALLY, MR. SHARIF, I... UH... PUBLISH AL KHAN MAGAZINE.
AL KHAN?!! ONE OF YOUR JOURNALISTS HAS BEEN GRILLING ME! HER NAME IS NADA SOMETHING!
UM... UH... I... UH... DON'T SPEND MUCH TIME IN THE NEWSROOM!
COME ON, YOU MUST KNOW HER! SHE HAS LONGISH, THICK BLACK HAIR; SHE WEARS A LOOSE-FITTING COMMUNIST-STYLE BUSINESS SUIT; AND SHE HAS THAT LOOK IN HER EYES....
...LIKE SHE WOULD KILL SOMEONE WITH HER BARE HANDS IF SHE DISCOVERED THEY WERE HIDING A SECRET FROM HER!
EXCUSE ME!
© 2008. Tarek Shahin. www.alkhancomics.com

15 October 2008

SO ASHRAF SHARIF TURNED OUT TO BE LEILA'S FATHER?!
LEILA, THE GIRL YOU'RE SEEING? WHAT ARE THE ODDS?!
AND HE THREATENED TO BAN ME FROM SEEING LEILA IF I DON'T CONTROL NADA!
NADA HAS SPENT MONTHS INVESTIGATING THIS MAN'S BUSINESS PRACTICES. YOU CAN'T POSSIBLY...
I KNOW, YUNAN! I KNOW! WHAT DO I DO NOW?
DO YOU REALLY CARE ABOUT THIS LEILA? OR IS THIS STILL ABOUT YOUR PATHETIC, IMPURE INTENTIONS WITH HER?!
SHE'S THE ONE!
REALLY? OMAR, ARE YOU SURE?
YES, OF ALL THE GIRLS I'VE MET SINCE I RETURNED TO EGYPT, SHE'S THE ONE WHO HAS KEYS TO AN EMPTY APARTMENT!
© 2008. Tarek Shahin. www.alkhancomics.com

20 October 2008

YUNAN PHOTO FILES
OMAR IS BEING VERY STRANGE, BIG FALAFEL! HE SUDDENLY DECIDED TO FIGHT MY STORY AGAINST ASHRAF SHARIF FOR NO GOOD REASON! IT'S ALMOST AS IF HE DISCOVERED THEY WERE RELATED OR SOMETHING!
WELL...
WHAT? WHAT IS IT?! YOU KNOW SOMETHING?
YES, NADA, BUT I DON'T WANT TO BE THE ONE TO TELL YOU!
THERE'S SOMEONE ELSE WHO KNOWS!
A... CLOSE FRIEND OF YOURS!
© 2008. Tarek Shahin. www.alkhancomics.com

22 October 2008

ALO! ALRIGHT, LEILA, I'M IN ZAMALEK - ALMOST AT YOUR APARTMENT BUILDING!
SOON WE'LL BE TOGETHER!
HOLD ON, I'M GETTING A CALL ON THE OTHER LINE...
ALO! NADA?!
SHE'S HIS DAUGHTER?!!
LEILA IS ASHRAF SHARIF'S DAUGHTER?! THAT'S WHY YOU TRIED TO SABOTAGE MY INVESTIGATION INTO HIS BUSINESS?
OMAR, HOW COULD YOU?!
PLEASE UNDERSTAND, NADA! THERE WAS A TIME IN LONDON WHEN I HAD A DIFFERENT GIRL EVERY WEEK!
THE LAST SEVEN MONTHS, EVER SINCE I RETURNED TO CAIRO, HAVE BEEN LIKE AN ENDLESS DROUGHT! IN THIS CITY, IT'S NOT EASY TO FIND A GIRL AS UNINHIBITED AS LEILA!
THIS IS MY ONLY CHANCE!
I AM APPALLED!
I AM APPALLED!
PLEASE TELL ME THAT WAS AN ECHO AND THAT LEILA ISN'T STILL ON THE LINE!
© 2008. Tarek Shahin. www.alkhancomics.com

23 October 2008*

WELCOME TO ANOTHER EDITION OF "LOCAL TALK." TONIGHT WE ARE HONORED TO WELCOME ON THE SHOW HIS EXCELLENCY DR. AMGAD GAD, MINISTER OF PROSPERITY. WE'LL BE DISCUSSING THE MAIN CHALLENGES FACING OUR COUNTRY.
OH, OMAR, I'M SO HAPPY WE'RE FINALLY TOGETHER, ALONE! BUT... I'M SO NERVOUS!
NO, NO, LEILA! DON'T BE NERVOUS! THIS IS GOOD! THIS IS ESHTA! THIS IS RIGHT!
NO! I CAN'T! I'M SORRY! I'M ONLY 29 YEARS OLD! I'M NOT READY TO BE A WOMAN YET!!
WHAT?!! YOU MEAN YOU'RE STILL A....?
MANY POTENTIAL INVESTORS WITH THE URGE TO PUMP LIQUIDITY ARE OFTEN SHOCKED TO FIND THAT EGYPT'S MOST ATTRACTIVE ASSETS REMAIN ENTIRELY UNTAPPED!
WHICH BRINGS US TO THE TOPIC OF OFFSHORE DRILLING.
© 2008. Tarek Shahin. www.alkhancomics.com

24 October 2008

OH, DEAR GOD, MOST POWERFUL. MY MISGUIDED FRIEND, OMAR, WAS IN PURSUIT OF AN UNHOLY RELATIONSHIP WITH A GIRL HE MET ON AN UNHOLY BEACH ON THE NORTH COAST OF EGYPT.
AND AFTER SEVERAL MONTHS OF PURSUIT, MY FRIEND WAS STRUCK BY THE KNOWLEDGE THAT, CONTRARY TO HIS WISHES AND EXPECTATIONS, THIS GIRL WOULD NOT BE TOUCHED BY ANY MAN OUTSIDE OF BLESSED MARRIAGE.
GOD, THIS IS SO CONFUSING! I DO NOT UNDERSTAND WHAT THIS INCIDENT CAN POSSIBLY MEAN!! WHAT LESSON IS TO BE LEARNED?
OH, THAT'S RIGHT. GOD WINS!
© 2008. Tarek Shahin. www.alkhancomics.com

28 October 2008**

HE DIDN'T SHOW UP TODAY EITHER! DID NADA REALLY FIRE OMAR FROM 'AL KHAN,' A MAGAZINE OWNED BY HIS FAMILY?! CAN SHE?!
APPARENTLY SHE CAN AND SHE DID.
AL KHAN
NADA, DO YOU THINK OMAR WILL EVER COME BACK?
I DON'T WANT TO HEAR THE NAME 'OMAR' EVER AGAIN! NOT AFTER WHAT HE DID!
BUT I DON'T WANT HIM TO RUIN OUR WORK MOOD EITHER! HOW ABOUT WE ALL GO TO LUNCH TODAY AT FELFELA? I'M DYING FOR A DISH OF THEIR ALEXANDRIA FUUL!
WHAT'LL IT BE, MISS NADA? YOUR USUAL? MISS NADA? YOUR USUAL? HUH? HUH?
COME ON, NADA! TALK TO THE MAN! IT'S NOT THE WAITER'S FAULT HIS NAME HAPPENS TO BE OMAR!
OMAR
© 2008. Tarek Shahin. www.alkhancomics.com

Notes by the author:

* "Eshta" in Arabic literally means "cream" but can mean "cool" in everyday dialect.

** 'Felfela,' adjacent to Tahrir Square in Cairo, did not pay me for this plug. I never asked.

29 October 2008

OMAR, WHAT HAPPENED BETWEEN YOU AND NADA? DID YOU HAVE A FALLING OUT REGARDING THE STRATEGY OF THE MAGAZINE? IS THAT WHY YOU HAVEN'T BEEN GOING THERE FOR DAYS? DID YOU DO SOMETHING WRONG? TALK TO ME! I'M YOUR MOTHER.

WELL, WHATEVER HAPPENED, IF YOUR FATHER WERE STILL WITH US, HE'D TELL YOU TO GET UP AND STAND ON YOUR FEET AGAIN!

EVEN YOUR LITTLE BROTHER MAGED WILL TELL YOU THAT.
YES, OMAR! I THINK YOU SHOULD STAND ON YOUR FEET AGAIN!

YOU'VE BEEN SITTING ON THE REMOTE FOR THREE DAYS!! PLEEEASE! STAND UP ON YOUR FEET FOR ONE SECOND!

30 October 2008

AL KHAN
NOVEMBER 2008
THE SOURCE OF ASHRAF SHARIF'S WEALTH?
REPORT BY: NADA SALEH

BITCH.
HELLO, MR. SHARIF! I'M HERE AS PER OUR APPOINTMENT.
AL KHAN

I HEARD YOU GOT KICKED OUT OF YOUR OWN PROPERTY! TELL ME, WHY DO YOU THINK YOU CAN HELP MY BID FOR ENECO WHEN IT GETS PRIVATIZED? OH, BY THE WAY, SORRY TO HEAR THAT YOU AND MY DAUGHTER BROKE UP!
AL KHAN

DID I EVER TELL YOU I USED TO BE AN INVESTMENT BANKER BEFORE I INHERITED 'AL KHAN'? HIRE ME AS YOUR ADVISOR AND YOU **WILL** WIN THE BID FOR ENECO!!
HAVE A SEAT, OMAR! YOU HAD ME AT HELLO!

31 October 2008

OMAR, WHAT'S A CREDIT CRUNCH?

WELL, MAGED, IT'S A SITUATION THAT ARISES FROM THE EXPANSION OF DEBT INSTRUMENTS IN THE FINANCIAL MARKETS WHEN THE UNDERLYING PHYSICAL ASSET IS LOSING FUNDAMENTAL VALUE.

IMAGINE SMOKING A JOINT BUT THERE'S NO FOOD IN THE FRIDGE.
OH, YOU MEAN IT'S LIKE A TOTAL COLLAPSE OF THE SYSTEM!!

1 November 2008

HAJJ SAYED, I ASKED YOU HERE TODAY BECAUSE I'VE DECIDED TO GIVE YOU A DISCOUNT ON THE MERCHANDISE YOU ORDERED.
THANKS, HAJJA FOLLA! BUT WHY WOULD YOU GIVE ME A DISCOUNT?!!
I'M EXTENDING A PROFESSIONAL COURTESY! THE BOYS HAVE BEEN READING TO ME ABOUT THIS WORLD CREDIT CRUNCH CRISIS THING AND SOME ACADEMICS ARE SAYING THAT IT'S ALREADY AFFECTING LOCAL EGYPTIAN BUSINESSES! HAVEN'T YOU BEEN AFFECTED?
UM... HAVE YOU?
HAVE YOU?
IF I TOLD YOU I WAS WOULD YOU GIVE ME THE DISCOUNT?
SURE, BUT THIS TIME, PAY IN CASH! YOU KNOW HOW IT IS WITH THIS CREDIT CRUNCH!
© 2008. Tarek Shahin. www.alkhancomics.com

5 November 2008

Dear readers,
At the time of this writing, we have yet to know the winner of the U.S. presidential election.
Therefore, two 'Al Khan' comic strips have been written; one for if Barack Obama wins and one for if John McCain wins.
We have chosen, regardless of the outcome of the election, to run both: the Obama one today and the McCain one tomorrow.
MAN, I FEEL SO HAPPY!! THIS WIN WILL BRING REAL CHANGE!
I'M GLAD OUR GUY EMERGED VICTORIOUS!
YEAH, I'M GLAD ABU TREIKA SCORED THAT SECOND GOAL!!
IF HE HADN'T, EGYPT WOULD HAVE FACED FOUR MORE YEARS OF NO PROGRESS!
That's right, America!
Stop arrogantly assuming that everyone in the world is following your election.
We have our own ~~elections~~ interests.
Thank you, 'Al Khan'
© 2008. Tarek Shahin. www.alkhancomics.com

6 November 2008

YES!!!! THE MUSLIM HAS WON! THE MUSLIM HAS WON!
ANWAR, YOU ARE MISTAKEN! BARACK OBAMA IS NOT A MUSLIM!
OBAMA NEXT U.S. PRESIDENT
OF COURSE HE IS, BROTHER LEVY! HE ONLY PRETENDED NOT TO BE DURING THE CAMPAIGN IN ORDER TO GET THE VOTE OF THE JEWISH LOBBY!
SPEAKING OF WHICH, YOU KNOW WHAT THIS MEANS, DON'T YOU? JERUSALEM IS OURS!!
I THINK YOU HAVE A RATHER MISGUIDED PERCEPTION ABOUT HIS PLAN!
BARACK OBAMA?
GOD!
© 2008. Tarek Shahin. www.alkhancomics.com

13 November 2008

THIS IS IT, CHIEF RIFAI!! THEY ARE GOING TO SELL THE COMPANY! WE'LL LOSE OUR JOBS!
FELLOW ENECO WORKERS! THIS IS OUR MOMENT OF RECKONING!! IF WE CANNOT FEED OUR KIDS, THEN WE MUST REVOLT!!
ENGINEERING NILE EGYPTIAN COMPANY (ENECO.)
GATHER YOUR TOOLS!! FORM A UNITED STAND! AND IF YOU SEE THE RIOT POLICE, COVER YOUR HEADS!...
WE'RE TOO LATE, YUNAN! THE WORKERS ARE REVOLTING!
THEY'RE BEYOND LISTENING TO JOURNALISTS NOW! WE NEED TO SPEAK TO THEM FROM WITHIN!
WHAT DO YOU MEAN "FROM WITHIN?"
AND IF YOU SEE THE STATE SECURITY FORCES...
COME ON, YUNAN! MINGLE WITH THE WORKERS!
NADA, YOU'RE INSANE! WE'LL GET HURT!
...COVER YOUR ANUSES!

14 November 2008

OH NO! YA LAHWY! THEY'RE PRIVATIZING ENECO!! WE'RE GOING TO LOSE OUR JOBS!!! HEY, WHO ARE YOU?! DO YOU WORK HERE?
HUH? ER... I'M YUNAN. I...ER... WORK THE NIGHT SHIFT!
OH? WITH HASSANEIN OR WITH AHMADEIN?
HUH? ER... UH... HASSANEIN. NO. AHMADEIN. NO. HASSANEIN. DEFINITELY HASSANEIN.
HASSANEIN PROPOSED TO ME! IT MADE AHMADEIN ANGRY. WHAT SHOULD I DO?
HUH? I DON'T KNOW, OK? UH... IT SEEMS YOU CARE MORE ABOUT AHMADEIN. SO GO WITH AHMADEIN!
AHMADEIN IS MY BROTHER!
HASSANEIN. DEFINITELY HASSANEIN!
ENGINEERING NILE EGYPTIAN COMPANY (ENECO.)

15 November 2008

I'M STANDING HERE AT THE SITE OF "ENGINEERING NILE EGYPTIAN COMPANY (ENECO)", WHERE THOUSANDS OF WORKERS ARE PROTESTING THE PRIVATIZATION OF THE CENTURIES-OLD COMPANY.
WHAT PROTESTS?!
I'M JOINED BY AN OFFICIAL FROM THE MINISTRY OF INTERIOR... 'WHAT PROTESTS?' THE PROTESTS BY THE ENECO WORKERS WHO ARE FACING UNEMPLOYMENT!
WHAT UNEMPLOYMENT?!
YOU'RE NOT EXPECTING ANGER? THEN HOW DO YOU EXPLAIN THE STATE SECURITY CAR CARRYING RIOT POLICE FORCES?
WHAT CAR?

17 November 2008

MY NAME IS NADA SALEH, I'M A JOURNALIST AND I CAME TO WARN YOU, CHIEF RIFAI, TO CALL OFF THE PROTESTS!
WELL, I DON'T KNOW HOW YOU SNEAKED INTO THE ENECO PLANT, WOMAN, BUT THE WORKERS LISTEN ONLY TO ME!
BUT, CHIEF RIFAI, VIOLENCE ACHIEVES NOTHING! MY MAGAZINE IS TRYING TO INFLUENCE PUBLIC OPINION ABOUT THE PRIVATIZATION OF ENECO THROUGH WORDS!
WORDS DON'T PUT FOOD ON THE TABLE! THE WORKERS MUST REVOLT! AND DON'T WORRY, I HAVE EVERYTHING UNDER CONTROL!!
BUT IF THE WORKERS GET HURT, IT WILL BE ON YOUR...
MAN, THIS IS SILLY!!
I KNOW IT'S SILLY, BUT WHAT CAN WE DO?
CAN'T WE AT LEAST ALLOW THEM TO SPEAK DIRECTLY TO EACH OTHER?
ORDERS ARE ORDERS!
© 2008. Tarek Shahin. www.alkhancomics.com

18 November 2008*

SALAM ALAIKOM, HASSA FOLLA! MY NAME IS OMAR SHUKRI. I'M ADVISING ASHRAF SHARIF ON HIS BID FOR ENECO! I'M HERE TO MAKE A PROPOSITION!
THAT MAN LOST MONEY IN BAD INVESTMENTS. HIS BID WILL BE NO MATCH FOR MINE! I DON'T NEED HIM!
FINE! DON'T CONSIDER IT A COLLABORATION. I HEAR YOU'RE A CHARITABLE LADY. THINK OF IT AS AN EID GIFT!
EID IS IN DECEMBER! THAT'S NOT FOR ANOTHER THREE WEEKS!
I'M SERIOUS, HASSA FOLLA! WHAT CAN I DO TO GET YOU TO HELP ME?!
YOU CAN GIVE US THAT SUIT! I WANT MY BOY HERE TO WEAR DARK THREADS WHEN WE MEET THE MINISTER! THINK OF IT AS AN EID GIFT!
THIS IS AN 800 DOLLAR ARMANI SUIT! AND I THOUGHT EID WASN'T FOR ANOTHER THREE WEEKS!
THAT'S HOW LONG IT'LL TAKE TO TURN IT INTO A GALABIYA!
© 2008. Tarek Shahin. www.alkhancomics.com

21 November 2008

YOU KNOW I'M A STRONG WOMAN, BIG FALAFEL! IF THE PRICE I HAVE TO PAY FOR GETTING INVOLVED WITH THE FACTORY WORKERS IS A FEW DAYS IN PRISON, THEN SO BE IT!
WHO'S BIG FALAFEL?
OH, HE'S A FRIEND I SHARE EVERYTHING WITH. I GUESS BEING AWAY FROM HIM IS MAKING ME DELUSIONAL!
YOU'RE NOT DELUSIONAL, NADA! I CAN SENSE YOUR HARDSHIP. HANG IN THERE! YOU ARE A STRONG WOMAN, NADA!
WHO'S NADA?
© 2008. Tarek Shahin. www.alkhancomics.com

Notes by the author:

* 'Galabiya,' is a traditional Arabic/African dress - like the one worn by Folla's boy.

22 November 2008

ALRIGHT, BOY, HERE'S ONE MILLION POUNDS, AS AGREED.
OMAR, MAKE SURE HE GETS THE OTHER MILLION WHEN HE DELIVERS THE INFORMATION ABOUT HAJJA FOLLA'S BID.
OF COURSE, MR. SHARIF. OH, JUST ONE MORE THING, MR. SHARIF. SMILE!!!

WHAT?
SNAP

GOT YOU!
YUNAN! WHAT TOOK YOU SO LONG?!
WHAT'S GOING ON?!

THAT GUY WAS BLINKING!
YEAH, THAT WOULD'VE MADE THE PHOTO TOTALLY INADMISSIBLE IN COURT!
WHAT HAVE YOU DONE?!!

24 November 2008*

ASHRAF SHARIF, YOU'RE UNDER ARREST FOR BRIBERY AND ATTEMPTING TO TAMPER WITH A GOVERNMENT AUCTION!
YOU'RE NOT ONE OF HAJJA FOLLA'S BOYS?!! YOU WERE UNDER-COVER?! NO! NO!!

THANK YOU FOR YOUR HELP, MR. OMAR! WE'VE BEEN INVESTIGATING THIS MAN FOR YEARS!
THANK YOU, SIR, FOR GIVING YUNAN THE PHOTO SCOOP!

THIS ISN'T OVER, OMAR! I'LL BE BACK TO RUIN YOUR LIFE AND THE LIVES OF EVERYONE AT THAT MAGAZINE OF YOURS! I HAVE CONNECTIONS!
HAVEN'T YOU HEARD? EGYPT PROSECUTES EVERYONE NOW! EVEN WEALTHY BUSINESS-MEN!

YEAH, BUT MY CONNECTIONS ARE MEMBERS OF THE NATIONAL DEMOCRATIC PARTY, AND VERY CLOSE TO THE PRESIDENT!
HAVEN'T YOU HEARD?

25 November 2008

SHEIKH AZIZ, HAJJA FOLLA, AS MINISTER OF PROSPERITY, I REGRET TO INFORM YOU THAT AFTER THE WORKERS' RIOTS, WE'VE DECIDED TO CANCEL THE PRIVATIZATION OF ENECO. YOU EACH PUT SIZEABLE BIDS, BUT I GUESS THE WORKERS' UNION WOULD RATHER THEY KEEP THEIR STEADY JOBS THAN TO SELL THEIR 5% STAKE IN THE COMPANY!

I'LL TAKE IT, YOUR EXCELLENCY. I'LL BUY THE WORKERS' 5% STAKE FOR THE SAME TOTAL BID AMOUNT!
WHAT?! YOU WANT TO PAY THE SAME AMOUNT FOR 5% THAT YOU WOULD'VE PAID FOR 100% OF THE COMPANY?! WHY, HAJJA FOLLA?

WIN-WIN! THE GOVERNMENT GETS THE PROCEEDS IT HAD BUDGETED FOR, I GET TO SEE 10,000 UNPRODUCTIVE WORKERS BECOME MOTIVATED ENTREPRENEURS AND ENECO'S WORKER BASE GETS RECYCLED! AND I WANT A SEAT ON ENECO'S BOARD TO OVERSEE THE COMPANY'S PROGRESS!

JUST LIKE THAT? YOU'RE OFFERING A GESTURE OF SUCH MAGNITUDE WITHOUT EVEN MAKING THEM NAME SOMETHING AFTER YOU?
GOOD POINT! I ALSO WANT SHEIKH AZIZ SQUARE TO BE RENAMED EGYPT SQUARE.

Notes by the author:

* Wishful thinking at the time.

26 November 2008

THEY LET ME GO WITH THE REST OF THE FACTORY WORKERS! I'M FREE, YUNAN!
WELL, THERE'S SOME MORE GOOD NEWS, NADA! ASHRAF SHARIF IS OFFICIALLY UNDER INVESTIGATION!
PRISON
REALLY? FINALLY!! HOW?!
WITH SOME HELP! YOU CAN THANK....
WHAT'S HE DOING HERE?!
NADA, I WANT TO APOLOGIZE FOR WHAT I.... HEY, WHY ARE YOU DRESSED IN A WORKER'S UNIFORM?
HA HA HA HA HA HA HA HA HA! LOOK AT NADA IN HER CUTE WORKING CLASS OVERALLS! HA HA HA HA!
NOT THE CLIMATIC REUNION I HAD IN MIND!

27 November 2008

SO OMAR ONLY PRETENDED TO BE WORKING FOR SHARIF, BUT YOU GUYS WERE ACTUALLY WORKING WITH THE POLICE TO BRING HIM DOWN? YUNAN, WHY DIDN'T YOU TELL ME?
YOU WERE SO CONSUMED WITH YOUR ANGER AT OMAR, I JUST DIDN'T THINK YOU'D UNDERSTAND, NADA!
SO OMAR DOES HAVE A GOOD BONE IN HIM! WHAT HAPPENED, OMAR? I THOUGHT YOU SAID EVERYTHING WAS FOR SALE!
EVERYTHING, NOT EVERYONE!
FAIR ENOUGH.
MAY I COME BACK NOW TO WORK AT THE MAGAZINE MY GRANDFATHER OWNS?
WELCOME BACK, OMAR!
PROUD TO BE YOUR COLLEAGUE, NADA! ALWAYS HAVE BEEN.

2 December 2008

WORKERS OF 'ENGINEERING NILE EGYPTIAN COMPANY (ENECO),' MY RICH ACQUISITION OF YOUR UNION'S 5% STAKE WILL MAKE EACH AND EVERYONE OF YOU VERY WEALTHY!
MY ONLY CONDITION IS THAT YOU LEAVE THE COMPANY AND THAT WITHIN TWO YEARS EACH OF YOU WILL HAVE STARTED YOUR OWN BUSINESS!
LONG LIVE HAJJA FOLLA!!
ENECO.
AND YOU CAN CHOOSE ANY BUSINESS IDEA YOU WISH!
YEAAAAH!
EXCEPT CIGARETTE KIOSKS!
BOOOOOOooo!

3 December 2008

WOW! WHAT HASSA FOLLA DID FOR THE WORKERS OF ENECO IS UNBELIEVABLE, NADA!
IT SHOWS BUSINESS AND SOCIAL INNOVATION! SHE'S GOT THE STUFF OF A TRUE EGYPTIAN WOMAN!
WHAT'S THAT?
COME ON, OMAR! WHAT'S THAT THING THAT ALL TRUE EGYPTIAN WOMEN HAVE?!
IT STARTS WITH A 'C.'
CELLULITE?
COURAGE!!
WHAT IS WRONG WITH YOU?!

© 2008. Tarek Shahin. www.alkhancomics.com

10 December 2008

ALRIGHT EVERYONE, THIS WEEK'S DEADLINES FOR THE NEWS STORIES AND THE EDITORIALS ARE STILL ON!
I WANT THEM ON MY DESK.
NOW, I KNOW IT'S THE FIRST DAY BACK AFTER THE EID HOLIDAY...
...AND I KNOW THE IDEA OF BRIDGING THE EID BREAK WITH THE WEEKEND CAN BE TEMPTING TO SOME...
...SO I GUESS I'LL SEE YOU ALL NEXT WEEK.

© 2008. Tarek Shahin. www.alkhancomics.com

12 December 2008

NADA! YOU DIDN'T TELL ME YOU SPENT A WEEK IN PRISON LAST MONTH!
I GOT TOO CLOSE TO A WORKERS' RIOT!
IT'S NO BIG DEAL, MOTHER!
BESIDES, EVEN IF I'D TOLD YOU, YOU WOULDN'T HAVE SPARED TIME AWAY FROM YOUR MOVIE SET!
NAME ONE TIME I WAS NOT THERE FOR YOU!
WHEN I WAS A GIRL, I FELL AT SCHOOL AND INJURED MY ARM! WHERE WERE YOU? SHOOTING ANOTHER MOVIE!
I TOOK YOU TO SEE A RUSSIAN DOCTOR THAT DAY!
DR. ZHIVAGO? HOW DID TAKING ME TO MEET OMAR SHARIF SUPPOSED TO HAVE MADE ME FEEL BETTER?!
I DON'T UNDERSTAND THE QUESTION.

© 2008. Tarek Shahin. www.alkhancomics.com

13 December 2008

MY FATHER SAYS HIS PHARMACY IS SUFFERING IN THE WAKE OF THIS ECONOMIC CRISIS!
I'M SURRISED, YUNAN! WHEN I USED TO ANALYZE MARKETS, WE USED TO CALL PHARMACEUTICALS A DEFENSIVE INDUSTRY!
WELL, HE SAYS PEOPLE ARE TAKING MORE HEALTH PRECAUTIONS TO BUY LESS MEDICINE!
TELL YOUR FATHER TO HAVE FAITH IN HIS BUSINESS. SEE, WE USED TO CALL THAT A LONG TERM VIEW.
AND IT LOOKS LIKE THE POVERTY IS WORSENING! PEOPLE AREN'T EVEN BUYING CONTRACEPTIVES!
IDIOTS! THEY THINK HAVING EVEN MORE KIDS WILL STRENGTHEN EGYPT'S ECONOMY?!
NO, THEY THINK IT WILL STRENGTHEN THE REVOLUTION.
AH, SEE, WE USED TO CALL THAT A NEAR TERM VIEW!

15 December 2008*

THAT'S WHERE HE USED TO SIT, NADA! SELLING MAGAZINES AND BOOKS ON THE STREET UNTIL HE EVENTUALLY BECAME EGYPT'S BIGGEST BOOK PUBLISHER!
مكتبة مدبولي
MADBULI BOOKSHOP
OH, I'M SORRY, BIG FALAFEL. ARE YOU STILL MOURNING THE DEATH OF HAJJ MADBULI?
LAST WEEK I COULDN'T STOP CRYING!
BUT NOW I FEEL BETTER! IN FACT, THINKING ABOUT HIS LEGACY HAS INSPIRED ME.
IN WHAT WAY?
I WANT TO BE HIM WHEN I GROW UP.
HAJJ MADBULI: 1938-2008

16 December 2008

FELLOW BROTHERS AND SISTERS, AS MINISTER OF PROSPERITY, I WOULD LIKE TO GIVE YOU ALL COMFORT THAT, ALTHOUGH THERE ARE CHALLENGES AHEAD, EGYPT'S ECONOMY STANDS OUT AS RESILIENT AS WE FURTHER OUR DEMOCRATIC SYSTEM.
MISSED!
POINK!
POINK!
MISSED AGAIN!
IS THAT REALLY NECESSARY?
SORRY, SIR! THE POST-BUSH-IRAQ INVASION-FAREWELL-VISIT-TRAINING IS MANDATORY FOR ALL CABINET MEMBERS!

Notes by the author:

* As a student I met Madbuly in his flagship bookstore near Tahrir Square. Inspirational.

17 December 2008

PEOPLE ARE ANGRY AT THE AZHAR SHEIKH FOR SHAKING HANDS WITH PERES! AND RIGHTFULLY SO, I SAY!
THAT'S EGYPT FOR YOU, BROTHER LEVY! YOU'RE A GOVERNMENT CLERIC IF YOU SAY BANK INTEREST IS NOT USURY AND THAT IT'S OK TO SHAKE HANDS WITH THE JEWS!
ANWAR, MAYBE THE SHEIKH SHOOK HANDS WITH HIM AS A GESTURE OF PEACE! ISN'T THAT WHAT ISLAM IS ALL ABOUT? PEACE?!
YES, OF COURSE IT IS!
SO LONG AS WE'RE WINNING!

© 2008. Tarek Shahin. www.alkhancomics.com

18 December 2008

OH! OMAR! COME SIT DOWN! I CAN'T BELIEVE YOU TWO HAVE NEVER MET. OMAR SHUKRI, THIS IS NOAH LEVY, MY NEW FRIEND FROM ENGLAND.
I HAVE TO GO SEE A PATIENT. I'LL BE BACK IN HALF AN HOUR.
HAMED
SO HOW LONG HAVE YOU KNOWN ANWAR?
SINCE I MOVED TO CAIRO, ABOUT SIX MONTHS AGO.
NOAH, I'M ONLY GOING TO BE HALF AN HOUR, SO PLEASE DON'T OFFER TO GET THE BILL TODAY! IT'S ON ME!
ALRIGHT, ANWAR! IF YOU INSIST!
QAHWA HAMED
AND WHEN DO YOU PLAN ON TELLING HIM YOU'RE JEWISH?
STILL WORKING ON THAT, MATE.

© 2008. Tarek Shahin. www.alkhancomics.com

20 December 2008

NADA, THAT BUS CRASH THAT KILLED AROUND 60 PEOPLE IN THE SOUTH... HERE'S THE SECOND BATCH OF PHOTOS I TOOK. BUT I HAVE TO WARN YOU, THE IMAGES ARE DISTURBING!
OH MY GOD, YUNAN! THESE PHOTOS ARE A LOT MORE GORY THAN THE FIRST BATCH! LOOK AT THEIR FACES!!! THIS IS BEYOND DISTURBING! I FEEL LIKE THROWING UP!
I TOLD YOU!
OK, I'VE DECIDED TO RUN THE FIRST BATCH - THE ONE WITH PHOTOS OF THE VICTIMS' BODIES.
THIS SECOND BATCH - THE ONE WITH PHOTOS OF THE MINISTRY OFFICIALS TRYING TO LAY THE FULL BLAME ON THE DRIVERS... URGHHH! WE WON'T PRINT THOSE!

© 2008. Tarek Shahin. www.alkhancomics.com

24 December 2008

IT WAS AN INSANE YEAR, OMAR.
WELL, AT LEAST I'LL START THE NEW YEAR AFTER HAVING SETTLED BACK IN CAIRO.
YOU STILL MISS LONDON?
WHAT DO I ALWAYS SAY, NADA?
EGYPT IS MY LADY, CAIRO'S MY LITTLE GIRL.
YEAH, I'VE BEEN MEANING TO TELL YOU THAT LINE IS SWEET, BUT IT DOESN'T MAKE ANY SENSE! WHAT DO YOU MEAN YOUR "LITTLE GIRL?!"
YOU KNOW, WITH THE ADORABLE FEATURES AND THE CURIOUS BABY STEPS...
...AND THE CONSTANT SHOUTING AND SCREAMING!
FIN
النهاية
ALKHAN
SERIES TWO STARTS
3 JANUARY 2009
MY THANKS TO ALL READERS

25 December 2008

Al Khan
The Comic Strip by Tarek Shahin
SERIES TWO STARTS
3 JANUARY 2009
THANK YOU ALL FOR READING

31 December 2008

Al Khan
SERIES TWO STARTS
3 JANUARY 2009

PART TWO
Project Love

6 May 2009

THE MINISTRY OF PROSPERITY IS BEING CRITICIZED FOR THE "UNNECESSARY" SLAUGHTER OF THE PIGS, YOUR EXCELLENCY!
YOU THINK I DON'T KNOW THAT THIS IS A HUMAN-TO-HUMAN HYBRID VIRUS?! BUT WE HAD TO DEMONSTRATE SOME ACTION!
WE CAN'T POSSIBLY SLAUGHTER ALL THE SICK PEOPLE IN EGYPT!
YES, SIR, WE WOULDN'T DO THAT!
YES! WE CAN'T!
SIR... YOU MEAN WOULDN'T, RIGHT?
I WOULDN'T SPECULATE.

8 January 2009

THE LEBANESE, THE YEMENIS, EVEN THE INDONESIANS, THEY ALL THINK EGYPT IS FAIR GAME, ASSAULTING OUR EMBASSIES LIKE THAT!

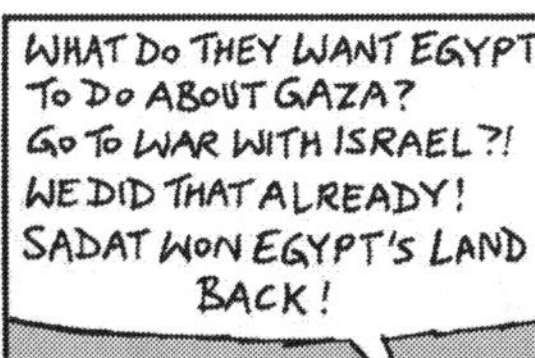
WHAT DO THEY WANT EGYPT TO DO ABOUT GAZA? GO TO WAR WITH ISRAEL?! WE DID THAT ALREADY! SADAT WON EGYPT'S LAND BACK!

NADA, WHEN WILL THEY REALIZE THAT SADAT WAS A GENUINE HERO FOR THE PEOPLE?
OMAR, WHEN WILL YOU REALIZE THAT SADAT WAS A GENUINE DESERTER OF ARAB UNITY?

SO WE'RE IN AGREEMENT!!

12 January 2009

NADA, I DON'T SEE WHY WE SHOULD STAY IN RAFAH! I TOOK ALL THE PHOTOS WE NEED FOR THIS WEEK'S ISSUE.
ALL EXCEPT ONE!

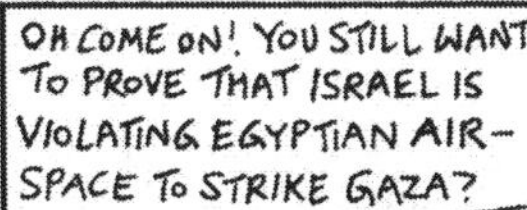
OH COME ON! YOU STILL WANT TO PROVE THAT ISRAEL IS VIOLATING EGYPTIAN AIR-SPACE TO STRIKE GAZA?

WHEN IT HAPPENS AGAIN WE'LL BE HERE TO CAPTURE IT ON FILM!
ISRAEL AND EGYPT BOTH DENIED IT HAPPENED!
YUNAN, I DON'T CARE WHAT THEY SAY! WE HAVE A COMMITMENT TO BRING OUR READERS THE TRUTH!

THAT'S WHAT I'M SAYING! ISRAEL AND EGYPT BOTH DENIED IT! OUR READERS DON'T NEED MY CAMERA TO PROVE IT DID HAPPEN! LET'S JUST GO HOME.

13 January 2009

ANWAR! ANWAR? AGAIN?! WHAT IS IT THIS TIME?!
I CAN'T AISHA! I CAN'T! I KEEP THINKING ABOUT THOSE POOR PEOPLE DYING IN GAZA!

THEY'RE ALLOWING DOCTORS VIA RAFAH. I'LL GO VOLUNTEER IN THE MORNING.
ANWAR, YOU'LL GET YOURSELF KILLED!!

WOULD YOU RATHER BE THE WIFE OF A COWARD OR THE WIDOW OF A MARTYR?
YOUR CHILDREN NEED A FATHER.

THE CHILDREN NEED A ROLE MODEL WHO WILL FORGO THE PLEASURES OF THIS FINITE WORLD!
THEY HAVE ME!!

14 January 2009

YOUR EXCELLENCY, AREN'T YOU UPSET WITH WHAT ROBERT FISK WROTE ABOUT EGYPT'S STANCE ON THE ISRAELI ASSAULT ON HAMAS?
WHO'S ROBERT FISK? I'M THE MINISTER OF PROSPERITY. READING IS NOT IN MY JOB DESCRIPTION.

BRITISH JOURNALIST. HE WROTE, "BREAK OFF RELATIONS WITH ISRAEL AND EGYPT'S ECONOMIC FOUNDATIONS CRUMBLE..." "THE ROTTEN STATE OF EGYPT IS TOO POWERLESS AND TOO CORRUPT TO ACT."

WHAT?! HOW DARE HE? THOSE FOREIGN JOURNALISTS CAN'T BE ALLOWED TO USE SUCH LANGUAGE!!

"CRUMBLE" IS SUCH A STRONG WORD.

15 January 2009

THE THINGS I'VE SEEN, BIG FALAFEL. HORRIBLE THINGS!
WHAT DID YOU EXPECT, NADA? IT'S A BLOOD BATH OUT THERE!

I DON'T TRUST THE OFFICIAL COUNT OF THE VICTIMS.
THE REAL NUMBER WILL SHOCK YOU!

THERE CANNOT BE PEACE WITHOUT EQUALITY AND HUMAN DIGNITY.
LET'S JUST PRAY THIS CONFLICT ENDS SOON...

I SAW IT FIRST!
OVER MY DEAD BODY!!
...BECAUSE THIS IS GETTING RIDICULOUS!
BUTANE COOKING GAS
EGP 8
EGP 20
Out of Stock

17 January 2009

OMAR, FOR THE LAST TIME, NADA IS THE CHIEF EDITOR!! YOU DON'T GET TO EDIT MY COVER STORY!!
AS THE PUBLISHER, I WOULD LIKE 'AL KHAN' TO BE MORE REFINED THAN OTHER NEWS MEDIA IN THE MIDDLE EAST.

I REPORTED ON THE MORE THAN 1,000 GAZANS MARTYRED IN THE ISRAELI STRIKE! YOU THOUGHT IT WAS BELOW PAR?
ALIA, I HAD A PROBLEM WITH THE TERM "MARTYRED."

HOW... HOW COULD YOU EVEN...? ALL THOSE POOR WOMEN AND CHILDREN!
I FEEL SORRY FOR INNOCENT VICTIMS, BUT IN JOURNALISM, 'DEAD' IS FACT. 'MARTYRED' IS OPINION.

OMAR, I HONESTLY THINK YOUR SOUL WILL BURN IN HELL!
SEE? YOU THINK BUT YOU DON'T KNOW! THAT'S ALL I'M SAYING!!

21 January 2009

WHERE HAVE YOU BEEN, BROTHER LEVY?! I NEEDED YOU THESE PAST FEW WEEKS!
I WAS BACK HOME IN ENGLAND FOR THE HOLIDAYS. WHAT'S UP?
OH, NOTHING, NOAH! JUST A LITTLE MASSACRE INVOLVING ISRAEL AND THE GAZANS!
YEAH, SHAME ABOUT THAT, MATE!
OMAR AND EVEN MY WIFE, AISHA, STOOD IN THE WAY OF MY RAGE! I NEEDED YOU TO HELP ME THROUGH THIS, BROTHER LEVY.
I'M HERE NOW, ANWAR.
WE CAN ONLY TRY TO IMAGINE HOW MANY INNOCENT MUSLIMS DIED!
DON'T BE TOO HARD ON YOURSELF, ANWAR. OF THE THIRTEEN PEOPLE KILLED, HOW MANY MUSLIMS COULD THERE HAVE BEEN?
© 2009. Tarek Shahin. www.alkhancomics.com

22 January 2009

NADA, YOU CAN NO LONGER ACCUSE ME OF BEING A SHALLOW ACTRESS! I'M GOING TO MAKE A MOVIE ABOUT THE GAZA WAR!
MOTHER, THAT'S CALLED CAPITALIZING ON THE MISERY OF OTHERS.
FOR YOUR INFORMATION, I PLAN TO DEDICATE ALL THE PROCEEDS TO THE PALESTINIANS!
SINCE WHEN DO YOU CARE? OK, TELL ME HOW YOU PLAN TO TRANSFER THE PROCEEDS.
TRANSFER?
AND HOW WILL YOU ALLOCATE THE MONEY? TO THEIR FOOD NEEDS? TO THEIR SCHOOLS?
NO, NO, LIKE, TO THEIR MEMORY!
NAHED HABIB
CREAMY SEWAGE
© 2009. Tarek Shahin. www.alkhancomics.com

23 January 2009*

YOUR EXCELLENCY, THE RULING PARTY IS ERASING THE FOUNDATIONS UPON WHICH THIS REPUBLIC WAS FOUNDED!
THEY THREW AWAY NASSER'S IDEALS AND EGYPT IS NOW EXPORTING GAS TO ISRAEL ALMOST FOR FREE!
TO THE ZIONISTS, AFTER THEY DESTROYED GAZA AND MURDERED ALL THOSE PEOPLE!!
AS ALWAYS, THE LEFTIST OPPOSITION IS THE ONE THINKING OF THE PEOPLE!
HEY!!! THE NDP HAS ALWAYS PUT SOCIAL RESPONSIBILITY AT THE HEART OF ITS POLICIES!
OH YEAH?? AND HOW EXACTLY DOES GIVING AWAY GAS TO THE ZIONISTS FIT INTO YOUR "SOCIALIST" IDEOLOGY?
"FROM EACH ACCORDING TO HIS ABILITY TO EACH ACCORDING TO HIS NEED!" -KARL MARX
© 2009. Tarek Shahin. www.alkhancomics.com

Notes by the author:

* NDP: The National Democratic Party which had reigned Egypt for three decades.

24 January 2009

BROTHERS AND SISTERS, WELCOME TO "THE UNITED." I'M YASSER YOUSRY.
AS LEFTIST MP, I HAVE SPENT THE LAST FEW WEEKS EXPOSING THE RULING PARTY IN THE HOUSE OF PARLIAMENT...

EGYPT'S FAILURE TOWARDS THE PALESTINIANS IN THE FACE OF THE CRIMINAL ISRAELI ASSAULT HAS BEEN CREATIVELY DESCRIBED BY THE STATE MEDIA AS A SUCCESSFUL TRUCE!

THE NDP HAS ONCE AGAIN USED THE CONTROLLED STATE MEDIA TO SELL US UTTER NONESENSE!
BUT I HAVE A MESSAGE TO THEM:
YOU CAN'T FOOL US ALL!

IF YOU THINK THE PUBLIC WILL ALLOW YOU TO USE PEACE TO END A WAR, THINK AGAIN!

27 January 2009

I'VE TRAVELLED ALL OVER IN SEARCH FOR THE MAN I LOVE... FOR YOU, YUNAN...

HHHHH!! WHO? WHAT?!

HEY!!! BABA! MAMA! I'M PAST THE AGE OF 40! PLEASE GIVE ME SOME SPACE IN MY OWN ROOM!
HABIBI, WERE YOU HAVING THAT SAME DREAM AGAIN?

I NEVER TOLD YOU I WAS HAVING ANY DREAMS!
YUNAN, I CHANGE YOUR BED SHEETS EVERY MORNING.

28 January 2009

YUNAN, WELL DONE ON THIS WEEK'S COVER PHOTO! YOU REALLY... YUNAN?
SORRY, OMAR! I HAVEN'T BEEN SLEEPING PROPERLY. THIS DREAM KEEPS WAKING ME UP!

I'VE BEEN HAVING THESE DREAMS ABOUT... WELL, IT'S EMBARASSING AT MY AGE!
ABOUT WHAT? NAKED WOMEN?

EMBARASSING. I KNOW.
IT'S NOT EMBARASSING AT ALL! I USED TO HAVE ONE OF THOSE ALL THE TIME! ESPECIALLY BACK IN LONDON WHERE THE TEMPTATION WAS BIGGER.

REALLY? EVEN YOU?! WHAT DID YOU DO WHEN YOU WOKE UP?
I MADE HER BREAKFAST.

29 January 2009

YUNAN, YOUR PARENTS SAID YOU WANTED TO SPEAK TO ME ABOUT THE DREAMS YOU KEEP HAVING.
THIS WOMAN APPROACHES ME IN AN ACT OF LOVE. I WANT TO KNOW IF BY HAVING THIS DREAM I'M COMMITTING A SIN.

THIS WOMAN, ARE YOU MARRIED TO HER IN THE DREAM?
IT'S NOT CLEAR TO ME... I DON'T KNOW.

SO IT WOULD NOT BE A SIN IF I'M MARRIED TO HER IN THE CONTEXT OF THE DREAM?

IS SHE COPTIC?

2 February 2009

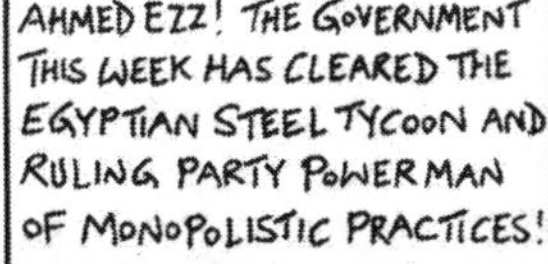
AHMED EZZ! THE GOVERNMENT THIS WEEK HAS CLEARED THE EGYPTIAN STEEL TYCOON AND RULING PARTY POWERMAN OF MONOPOLISTIC PRACTICES!

THE UNITED WITH YASSER YOUSRY

THEY SAID, WHEREAS THE PRICE OF STEEL DOUBLED LAST YEAR AMID HEIGHTENED BUILDING ACTIVITY, IT DROPPED BY HALF THIS YEAR DUE TO WEAKER GLOBAL DEMAND!

I THINK IT SAYS A LOT ABOUT THE EFFICIENCY OF THE FREE MARKET SYSTEM...
ESHTA! THIS GUY'S FINALLY STARTING TO MAKE SENS...

THAT IT ONLY WORKS HALF THE TIME!
ESHTA!

4 February 2009

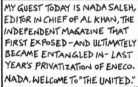

MY GUEST TODAY IS NADA SALEH, EDITOR IN CHIEF OF AL KHAN, THE INDEPENDENT MAGAZINE THAT FIRST EXPOSED - AND ULTIMATELY BECAME ENTANGLED IN - LAST YEAR'S PRIVATIZATION OF ENECO. NADA, WELCOME TO "THE UNITED."
THANK YOU, MR. YASSER.

NADA, EXPLAIN TO OUR VIEWERS HOW YOU USE YOUR MAGAZINE TO BATTLE OUR CORRUPT GOVERNMENT.
I DO NO SUCH THING! AL KHAN IS A SOURCE OF TRUTH! IT'S UP TO THE PEOPLE TO USE THAT TRUTH.

EXCUSE ME! ARE YOU SUGGESTING THE EGYPTIAN PEOPLE ARE LIKE ... LIKE SOME HERD OF BLIND SHEEP IN NEED OF A SHEPHERD?!
NO! NO! I WOULD NEVER INSINUATE SOMETHING INSULTING LIKE THAT!

INSULTING? NOT AT ALL! I'M HONORED!

5 February 2009

WE'RE BACK. SO, NADA, YOU ASSERT THAT YOU DON'T USE YOUR MAGAZINE AS A DIRECT COMBAT TOOL.
YES, MR. YASSER. THAT'S EXACTLY WHAT I'M SAYING.
UNITED

SO AS A MEMBER OF PARLIAMENT, I SHOULDN'T OPPOSE AND FIGHT THE GOVERNMENT'S DAMAGING POLICIES?
YOU CAN HAVE AN AGENDA AS A POLITICIAN BUT NOT AS A BROADCASTER. AN OPINION, BUT NOT AN AGENDA!

YOUNG LADY, DO YOU HAVE A HABIT OF TELLING PEOPLE HOW TO DO THEIR JOBS?
YES!! YES SHE DOES!!

SHUT UP, OMAR!!
WHO?

6 February 2009

NADA!! YOU LOOKED SO CUTE ON TELEVISION!!
I'M... I'M REALLY SURPRISED YOU WATCHED IT, BASMA!
I DIDN'T KNOW YOU WATCHED POLITICAL TALK SHOWS!

YOU'RE MY LITTLE SISTER, NADA. HOW COULD I MISS IT? WAIT! WHAT POLITICAL TALK SHOW?
YOU SAW ME BEING INTERVIEWED ON "THE "UNITED," RIGHT?

OH, NO, NO! MAMA WAS BEING INTERVIEWED ON THE FILM CHANNEL TO PROMOTE "CREAMY SEWAGE II" AND THEN SHE SHOWED THE AUDIENCE SOME OLD PHOTOS OF YOU WHEN YOU WERE A BABY!

OH MY GOD!! THAT'S EXACTLY HOW YOUR FACE LOOKED IN THE PHOTOS!

7 February 2009

YUNAN, I'M YOUR FATHER AND I'M GOING TO BE HONEST WITH YOU. YOU KEPT REJECTING OUR PLEA FOR YOU TO GET MARRIED AND NOW YOU'RE IN YOUR FORTIES HAVING FANTASIES ABOUT WOMEN IN YOUR SLEEP!

NOW, WHAT'S WRONG WITH MARIAN, GERGES'S DAUGHTER?
BABA, SHE'S DULL!! PLUS, I DON'T KNOW HER THAT WELL.

SON, LISTEN TO ME! I DIDN'T KNOW YOUR MOTHER THAT WELL BEFORE WE GOT MARRIED. BUT THROUGHOUT OUR LONG MARRIAGE I HAVE COME TO DISCOVER WONDERFUL AND EXCITING THINGS ABOUT HER WITH EVERY PASSING DAY!

YOU THINK I WILL EVENTUALLY DISCOVER SIMILAR THINGS ABOUT MARIAN?
I SERIOUSLY DOUBT IT. BUT AT YOUR AGE, YOU SHOULD TAKE WHAT YOU CAN GET!

9 February 2009

NADA! WHAT WAS THAT? YOU CAN'T APPEAR ON THE YOUSRY PROGRAM WITHOUT MY PERMISSION!
PERMISSION? YASSER WANTED TO INTERVIEW THE EDITOR IN CHIEF OF ALKHAN, NOT THE PUBLISHER!
WHY DID YOU EVEN GO? EVEN IF YOU ARE A LEFTIST, YOU CAN'T REALLY THINK THIS MAN HAS ANY CREDIBILITY!
YOU MAY HAVE NOTICED, OMAR, THAT I DESCRIBED HIM AS SENSATIONALIST ON THE AIR TO HIS FACE! I WAS VERY HARD ON HIM.
NOT NEARLY AS HARD AS YOU USUALLY ARE ON ME!
WELL, I MAY DISAGREE WITH YASSER'S METHODS BUT HIS HEART IS IN THE RIGHT PLACE!
OH, AS OPPOSED TO MY HEART WHICH IS....?
UNACCOUNTED FOR.
© 2009. Tarek Shahin. www.alkhancomics.com

10 February 2009

ALIA, TELL NADA I'M LEAVING EARLY TODAY. MY PARENTS WANT ME TO GET TO KNOW "THE BRIDE" THEY'RE FIXING ME UP WITH!
YUNAN, YOU'RE NOT SERIOUSLY GOING TO INDULGE THEM, ARE YOU?
ARRANGED MARRIAGES ARE THE VERY THING THAT IS WRONG WITH THIS COUNTRY! HOW CAN MODERN EGYPTIANS STILL EMBRACE THIS TIRED TRADITION?
HOW CAN TWO PEOPLE DECIDE THAT THEY BELONG TOGETHER IF THEIR RELATIONSHIP IS A PRODUCT OF WHAT IS ESSENTIALLY A PARENT-SUPERVISED SPEED DATING EVENT?
"AND HOW COULD IT BE THAT A VEILED WOMAN CAN HAVE SUCH SOCIALLY PROGRESSIVE VIEWS?" WONDERED OMAR PRESUMPTUOUSLY AS HE OVERHEARD IN SHOCK.
© 2009. Tarek Shahin. www.alkhancomics.com

12 February 2009*

SO, MARIAN, UH... WHO'S YOUR FAVORITE ARTIST? HAVE YOU READ ANY BOOKS RECENTLY?
LOLOLOLOLOLOLOLOLO-LOLOLOLOLOYYYY!!!
© 2009. Tarek Shahin. www.alkhancomics.com

Notes by the author:
* "...lolololoyy" is my attempt to spell out the Egyptian/Middle Eastern wedding chant.

16 February 2009

NADA? WHAT A SURPRISE TO SEE YOU HERE!
I THOUGHT I'D COME APOLOGISE FOR BEING A BIT HARSH ON YOU WHEN YOU INTERVIEWED ME.
OH, NO NEED. I'D INVITE YOU IN, BUT...
MR. YASSER, I DON'T LET SOCIETY TELL ME IF I CAN OR CANNOT ENTER A MAN'S HOME!
IT'S NOT THAT! IT'S THAT THEY'RE ABOUT TO AIR PRIME MINISTER NAZIF'S SPEECH ON THE ECONOMIC CRISIS, AND THERE'S GOING TO BE PROFANITY!
I NEVER HEARD NAZIF USE PROFANITY BEFORE!
NOT HIM! ME!!
I TAKE MY TEA WITH THREE SUGARS...
© 2009. Tarek Shahin. www.alkhancomics.com

17 February 2009

SO, NADA, IS IT TRUE YOU'RE THE DAUGHTER OF NAHED HABIB?
YES. THE SOULFUL FILM AND TV ACTRESS TURNED SOULLESS FILM AND TV STAR!
I TAKE IT YOU'RE NOT A FAN.
LONG STORY SHORT: MY FATHER WAS A PLAYWRIGHT WITH INTELLECT. SHE SOLD OUT. HE DIDN'T. SHE DROVE HIM AWAY!
AND YOU'VE SINCE RESENTED ALL THINGS MATERIAL AND SHUNNED ANY ROMANTIC RELATIONSHIP?
THAT'S RIGHT, MR. YASSER. AND YOU?
OH, I TOO FIND THAT FILTHY AND FUTILE!
WHICH? HER FILMS OR HER TV SERIES?
© 2009. Tarek Shahin. www.alkhancomics.com

19 February 2009

AND THIS IS MY PRIVATE LIBRARY... THE BOOKS THAT HAVE SHAPED HISTORY AND INFLUENCED MY POLITICS, MY PASSION FOR THE PEOPLE, MY STRIVE FOR ARAB DIGNITY.
I'VE READ THEM ALL!
AND THIS, NADA, IS WHAT KEEPS MY HOME WARM IN TIMES OF COLD AND LIT IN TIMES OF DARK! I CALL IT THE FREEDOM GALLERY.
WHAT DO YOU THINK?
THEY'RE GROTESQUE, MR. YASSER!
SERIOUSLY, I KNOW A PLACE THAT SELLS THEM IN COLOR!
© 2009. Tarek Shahin. www.alkhancomics.com

25 February 2009

BROTHERS AND SISTERS, THE POWERS THAT BE HAVE PLUNGED EGYPT INTO A MUD-PILE OF CAPITALIST CORRUPTION!
AFTER YEARS OF FUTILE ARGUMENT IN PARLIAMENT, I HAVE LOST THE ABILITY TO FIGHT ALONE FOR YOUR FUTURE!
THE UNITED WITH YASSER YOUSRY

WHICH IS WHY I WOULD LIKE TO INVITE YOU ALL TO JOIN 'PROJECT LOVE.'

STARTING TOMORROW MORNING, ALL SCHOOL AND UNIVERSITY STUDENTS ARE TO STAY AT HOME - I CALL ON YOU NOT TO ATTEND ANY CLASSES OR EXAMINATIONS!
TODAY'S YOUTH WILL NO LONGER BECOME TOMORROW'S GOVERNMENT TOOLS!

THAT'S RIGHT DEAR STUDENTS! STARTING TOMORROW, YOU ARE REQUIRED TO DO NOTHING.
NOW, WHO'S WITH ME?
THIS IS GOING TO BE VERY HARD WORK!...

26 February 2009

YASSER YOUSRY WENT ON LIVE TELEVISION AND CALLED ON EGYPT'S YOUTH TO BOYCOTT SCHOOLS AND UNIVERSITIES!! HE CALLS IT 'PROJECT LOVE!'
HE'S INSANE! COMPLETELY INSANE!

INTERESTING, NADA! I RECALL YOU SAYING HIS HEART WAS IN THE RIGHT PLACE!
YES, BUT THIS IS WAY OUT OF PROPORTION! I NEVER TOLD HIM TO... I MEAN... NEVERMIND.

"TOLD HIM?" NADA? DID YOU HAVE SOMETHING TO DO WITH THIS?
WHAT?! OMAR, WHAT DID YOU JUST ASK ME?! DON'T SAY ANOTHER WORD!!

SORRY, NADA. THAT WAS OUT OF LINE.
I SAID SHHHHH! I'M TRYING TO THINK ABOUT YOUR QUESTION!

28 February 2009

..ONE WEEK EARLIER...
THANK YOU FOR THE TEA, MR. YASSER. I SHOULD BE GOING.
LOOK AT OUR STREETS, NADA. DO YOU SEE THAT POOR FAMILY LIVING ON THE PAVEMENT?

THEY'RE LIVING IN SHIT, WHILE THE COUNTRY'S ELITE BASK IN THEIR WEALTH! IF I WERE PRESIDENT YOU'D NEVER SEE THAT!

IF I WERE PRESIDENT I'D MAKE SURE EVERYONE LIVED IN SHIT EQUALLY!

NADA...?

2 March 2009

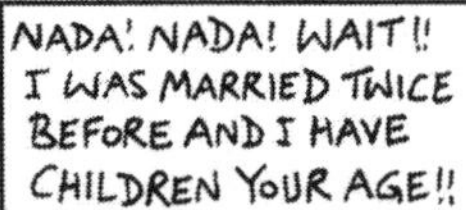
NADA! NADA! WAIT!! I WAS MARRIED TWICE BEFORE AND I HAVE CHILDREN YOUR AGE!!

I...I'M SORRY, MISTER YASSER! I DON'T KNOW WHAT CAME OVER ME! I SHOULD LEAVE RIGHT NOW!

WHERE ARE YOU GOING?!! WAS IT THE WHOLE 'I HAVE CHILDREN YOUR AGE' THING? I WAS TELLING YOU MORE ABOUT MYSELF! WOMEN DIG THAT! NO?

3 March 2009

NADA!! WHERE ARE YOU GOING? YOU CAN'T OFFER YOURSELF TO A MAN AND THEN JUST LEAVE LIKE THAT!! IT'S CRUEL! IMPOLITE EVEN!
GRRRR!

LISTEN YOU! I HAD A MOMENT OF WEAKNESS! GET OVER IT! SURE, FOR A SECOND I WAS TAKEN BY YOUR CHARM AND YOUR POLITICAL IDEOLOGY! BUT DON'T THINK FOR ONE SECOND I COULD EVER BE WITH SOMEONE LIKE YOU!

MR. YASSER, FOR ALL YOUR CHARISMA, YOU HAVE DONE NOTHING WITH YOUR LIFE! YOUR GREATEST ACHIEVEMENT AS AN OPPOSITION MEMBER OF PARLIAMENT WAS STARTING A TV TALKSHOW WHERE ALL YOU DO IS RANT SOME MORE!

WHAT HAVE YOU EVER DONE AS A POLITICIAN TO INSPIRE THE INDIVIDUALS IN THE COMMUNITY TO DO SOMETHING TO BETTER THEIR LIVES?
INDIVIDUALS? DO?! YOUNG CHILD, WHAT EXACTLY IS IT THAT YOU THINK SOCIALISM IS ABOUT?

4 March 2009

CAIRO: 1978
MR. PRESIDENT, WHY DID YOU DEPART FROM PRESIDENT NASSER'S PRINCIPLES?
BOY, YOU'RE A STUDENT! STOP MAKING NOISE AND BUILD AN ACTIVE LIFE!
NIVERSITY WELCOMES
DENT ANWAR SADAT

1992
YASSER, I'M LEAVING YOU! YOU HAVEN'T HAD A JOB SINCE UNIVERSITY! BEING AN "ACTIVIST" DOESN'T EXACTLY PUT FOOD ON THE TABLE! IF ALL YOU'LL DO IS OPPOSE THE GOVERNMENT, AT LEAST RUN FOR PARLIAMENT!!

2009: LAST WEEK
MR. YASSER, I CAN NEVER BE WITH SOMEONE LIKE YOU! AS AN OPPOSITION MEMBER OF PARLIAMENT, YOU'VE DONE NOTHING TO HELP PEOPLE BETTER THEIR LIVES!

PRESENT DAY
BROTHERS AND SISTERS, STUDENTS ARE TO SKIP SCHOOLS AND UNIVERSITIES IN AN EFFORT TO BATTLE CORRUPTION. WE HAVE A LOT TO DO! WELCOME TO PROJECT LOVE!
THE UNITED WITH YASSER YOUSRY

6 March 2009

THE INTERNATIONAL CRIMINAL COURT ISSUED AN ARREST WARRANT FOR BESHIR FOR WAR CRIMES IN DARFUR! HYPOCRISY!! WHAT ABOUT SHARON? WHAT ABOUT BUSH? THIS IS ALL ABOUT OIL!!
ON THE OTHER HAND, WHY IS EGYPT SO VOCAL ABOUT WANTING THIS ARREST WARRANT CANCELLED?
ANWAR, EGYPT HAS A VERY DELICATE AND COMPLICATED RELATIONSHIP WITH SUDAN.
EGYPT WANTS TO PROTECT ITS MOST VALUABLE OF TREASURES! IT'S A MATTER OF NATIONAL SECURITY!
THE NILE? WATER? THE "NEW OIL?" SAME THING!
NO, I MEANT ARAB EXCEPTIONALISM.
DARFUR

7 March 2009

YES, YOUR EXCELLENCY! MP YASSER YOUSRY'S TELEVISED CALL TO EGYPT'S YOUTH TO BOYCOTT THE EDUCATION SYSTEM IS A BLATANT SPIT ON THE GOVERNMENT'S FACE!
YES, YOUR EXCELLENCY! OF COURSE THE MINISTRY OF PROSPERITY CAN STRIP HIS PARLIAMENTARY IMMUNITY AND ARREST HIM FOR... WHAT'S THAT, SIR?
YES, SIR, OF COURSE I REALIZE THIS BOYCOTT HAS THE POTENTIAL OF SPREADING FURTHER ILLITERACY AND INTELLECTUAL ATROPHY AMONG OUR YOUTH. YES, SIR, I KNOW WE HAVE ELECTIONS IN TWO YEARS.
YES, SIR, OF COURSE WE CAN LET YOUSRY GO FOR NOW.

13 March 2009

AISHA!! WHY AREN'T ANY OF THE KIDS AT SCHOOL?!
I TRIED TAKING THEM, ANWAR! BUT THEY REFUSE TO GO!
APPARENTLY THEY NOTICED THE OLDER STUDENTS WEREN'T SHOWING UP AT SCHOOL! I THINK IT HAS SOMETHING TO DO WITH THAT BOYCOTT STARTED BY THAT MP, YASSER YOUSRY, LAST WEEK ON TELEVISION!
WHAT?!!
ARE THERE NO BOUNDARIES ANY MORE?! THIS CAN'T BE ALLOWED! I WILL NOT TOLERATE INDISCIPLINE IN MY HOME!!
DO I MAKE MYSELF CLEAR, AISHA?!
YES! I'M SORRY! I'M SORRY, ANWAR! I'LL NEVER WATCH TELEVISION AGAIN WITHOUT YOUR PERMISSION!!

14 March 2009

YUNAN, YOU CAN'T LEAVE AL KHAN MAGAZINE! YOU'RE OUR... NO, YOU'RE EGYPT'S BEST PHOTOGRAPHER!
WE CAN'T LOSE YOU, MAN!
THE PARTY'S OVER, GUYS. I'M GETTING OLDER AND NOW I'M GETTING MARRIED AND I NEED TO FIND A MORE STABLE JOB.
NADA, I HOPE YOU CAN UNDERSTAND MY POSITION.
YOU AND I HAVE BEEN BEST FRIENDS FOR YEARS. YOU'RE JUST GOING TO WALK AWAY?
YOU REALLY DO MEAN A LOT TO US, YUNAN.
IF YOU'RE CONCERNED ABOUT YOUR LIVELIHOOD I'M SURE OMAR CAN GIVE YOU A PAY RAISE.
NADA, I HOPE YOU CAN UNDERSTAND YUNAN'S POSITION.

18 March 2009

CAIRO: 1996
HELLO, MY NAME IS YUNAN SALIBA. I'D LIKE TO BE A PHOTOGRAPHER WITH AL KHAN MAGAZINE.
IS IT 'SALIBA' OR 'SALIB'? YOU DON'T LOOK LEBANESE, KID!
10 SEPTEMBER 2001
HELLO, MY NAME IS NADA. I JUST SEVERED ALL TIES WITH MY MOTHER AND WOULD LIKE TO BE A REPORTER WITH AL KHAN.
I'M YUNAN. I DOUBT THE EDITOR WILL OFFER YOU A JOB. IT'S BEEN A SLOW NEWS YEAR IN THE MIDDLE EAST.
2006
NADA, I TOOK ALL THE PHOTOS FROM THE PROTEST AGAINST THE DANISH PROPHET CARTOONS! LET'S GET OUT OF HERE!
I JUST GOT A MESSAGE FROM OUR PUBLISHER. HE'S CONSIDERING STEPPING DOWN NEXT YEAR AND BRINGING IN HIS GRANDSON- HIS NAME'S OMAR...
SEE, YUNAN? YOU AND AL KHAN HAVE A HISTORY. YOU AND I HAVE A HISTORY! YOU CAN'T LEAVE!!! AND DON'T SAY YOU'RE GETTING TOO OLD FOR THIS JOB!
I AM GETTING OLD, NADA! IN FACT, I CAN'T REMEMBER MOST OF THAT STUFF YOU JUST REMINISCED ABOUT!

19 March 2009

GOOD BYE, OMAR!
WE'RE GOING TO MISS YOU, YUNAN!
NADA...
I'M NOT TALKING TO YOU. DON'T BOTHER INVITING ME TO YOUR WEDDING.
WELL, IT'S BEEN AN INCREDIBLE THIRTEEN YEARS WITH AL KHAN. I WISH YOU ALL THE BEST OF LUCK.
AL KHAN MAGAZINE

20 March 2009

FIRST THERE WAS THIS SITUATION WITH MR. YOUSRY. AND THEN OUT OF NOWHERE YUNAN LEAVES AL KHAN. IT'S TOO MUCH FOR ME TO HANDLE, BIG FALAFEL!
EVERYTHING IS CHANGING.
WELL, THAT'S LIFE, NADA.
BELIEVE ME! I'VE BEEN WATCHING THE STREETS OF CAIRO FOR DECADES- LONG ENOUGH TO REALIZE THAT CHANGE CAN BE A GOOD THING!
HOW DO YOU USUALLY DEAL WITH CHANGE?
WHAT CHANGE?

21 March 2009

HOW COULD THE SUPREME COURT GRANT EGYPTIAN BAHAIS FULL CITIZEN RIGHTS?!! THIS IS AN OUTRAGE! WHO NEXT? HINDUS? BUDDHISTS? SHIITES?
BAHAI VICTORY
THAT'S IT, ANWAR!! I'M SICK OF YOU BEING SUCH A STEREOTYPE! I KNOW A LOT OF GOOD PEOPLE WHO ARE MUSLIM AND WHO BELIEVE IN RELIGIOUS FREEDOM WITH NO BOUNDARIES.
NO BOUNDARIES?! YOU'RE LYING, OMAR! I HAVE NEVER RUN INTO ANYONE AT THE FRIDAY PRAYER WHO THINKS THAT WAY.
I DIDN'T SAY THEY WERE GOOD MUSLIMS.

23 March 2009

SALAM ALAIKOM, DR. ANWAR. LET ME BUY YOU LUNCH. YOU LIKE KEBAB?
KEBAB? DR. ALY, LAST MONTH YOU COULDN'T AFFORD TO BUY BREAD!
HAVE YOU HEARD ABOUT THE NEW TEENAGE RAPISTS TERRORIZING THE WOMEN OF CAIRO?
NO.
AND YOU NEVER WILL! BECAUSE THEIR VICTIMS ARE TOO ASHAMED TO TALK ABOUT IT - EXCEPT TO BACK-ALLEY GYNECOLOGISTS LIKE ME.
AND BECAUSE I AM A GOD-FEARING MAN, I OFFER MY COUNSELLING FOR FREE.
IS THAT A NEW CAR?!
BUT I DO CHARGE THEM FOR MY SEWING KIT, THOUGH!

24 March 2009

SEE YOU, NADA! I'M OFF TO THE WEDDING PARTY IN HELIOPOLIS. DO I LOOK FAT IN THIS DRESS?
BASMA, WAIT! DON'T YOU THINK YOUR DRESS IS A BIT TOO REVEALING?

OK, I'M YOUR OLDER SISTER. YOU DON'T GET TO TELL ME THAT. AND MAYBE IF YOU HAD SOME HINT OF A SOCIAL LIFE YOU'D HAVE LESS TIME TO INTERFERE IN MINE!

I'M NOT KIDDING, BASMA! I KNOW THAT REMOTE AREA IN HELIOPOLIS... YOU'LL HAVE TO WALK A LONG DISTANCE ON FOOT AFTER YOU PARK. IT'S DANGEROUS!

THERE ARE MEN AROUND! THEY GET IDEAS!
SO... YOU'RE SAYING I **DON'T** LOOK FAT IN THIS DRESS.

26 March 2009

DID YOU READ THIS? A PROMINENT SHEIKH HAS JUST CLARIFIED HIS VIEWS ON FEMALE GENITAL MUTILATION BY ISSUING A FATWA AGAINST IT.
RIDICULOUS!
FGM
FATWA

WELL, SAY SOMETHING, OMAR! WHEN THE SCHOLARS DON'T BAN FGM, YOU'RE ANGRY. AND NOW WHEN THEY DO BAN FGM, YOU'RE ANGRY. I DON'T GET YOU!
FGM
FATWA

IT'S 2009!!!

FGM

FATWA

OH, I SEE YOUR POINT. I, TOO, DO NOT FAVOR FATWAS ISSUED IN HASTE.

27 March 2009

NADA! NADA! HELP ME!! HOLD ME!
BASMA? WHAT'S WRONG? WHAT HAPPENED?!

I WAS WALKING TOWARDS THE WEDDING PARTY... IT WAS DARK... THEY CAME OUT OF NO WHERE!! THREE GUYS.. MAYBE FOUR! THEY WERE YOUNG! COULD'VE BEEN STUDENTS! SO YOUNG! THEY... THEY...

BASMA, TELL ME EXACTLY WHAT THEY DID. THERE'S NOTHING TO BE ASHAMED OF. YOU HAVE TO GET CHECKED AT A HOSPITAL. BASMA, I'M YOUR SISTER! PLEASE... I BEG YOU...

PLEASE TALK TO ME!
TO BE CONTINUED...

28 March 2009

ALRIGHT, BASMA. I'M SKIPPING WORK TO TAKE YOU TO THE HOSPITAL AND THEN TO THE POLICE STATION.
THAT'S ALRIGHT, NADA. NO NEED.

BASMA, YOU WERE ASSAULTED ON THE STREET! YOU MAY HAVE BEEN RAPED!!
I... UH... ALREADY WENT TO THE HOSPITAL. THEY SAID NOTHING HAPPENED. I'M FINE.

WHEN?! WHY ARE YOU LYING TO ME? IF EVERY WOMAN IN EGYPT CHOOSES NOT TO REPORT AN ATTACK LIKE THIS THE PROBLEM ONLY GETS WORSE FOR OTHER WOMEN!

YOU KNOW WHAT? YOU ARE ABSOLUTELY RIGHT.
BUT.... WHAT ATTACK?

30 March 2009

OMAR, WE NEED TO LOOK INTO SEXUAL ASSAULTS.
ABSOLUTELY, NADA. REPORTS OF SEX CRIMES ON THE STREETS OF CAIRO ARE THE REASON MY EX-GIRLFRIEND, JANE, NEVER VISITS FROM LONDON!

GREAT! I'LL TELL ALL THE REPORTERS TO MAKE THAT OUR COVER STORY THIS WEEK.
COVER STORY? I WOULD THINK WE HAD MORE PRESSING TOPICS!

I THOUGHT YOU SAID REPORTS OF SEX CRIMES ARE THE REASON JANE NEVER VISITS CAIRO!

YES! **REPORTS** OF SEX CRIMES ARE THE REASON JANE NEVER VISITS CAIRO!
I REALLY MISS JANE!

31 March 2009

I SHOULDN'T HAVE TOLD BASMA HER DRESS WAS TOO REVEALING BEFORE SHE WENT OUT, BIG FALAFEL. NOW SHE THINKS IT'S HER FAULT SHE WAS ASSAULTED ON THE STREET!

BASMA SAID HER ATTACKERS LOOKED LIKE YOUNG STUDENTS. I'M STARTING TO SUSPECT THAT YASSER YOUSRY'S 'PROJECT LOVE' IS INDIRECTLY PLAYING A PART. ALL THOSE KIDS, SKIPPING SCHOOL, WITH NO ASPIRATIONS!

WISH ME LUCK TRYING TO LINK PROJECT LOVE TO THE TEEN RAPISTS.
NADA, A REPORTER WITH YOUR SKILLS AND INTEGRITY DOES NOT NEED LUCK!

YOU THINK SOCIETY WILL EVER BELIEVE IT WASN'T BASMA'S FAULT?
GOOD LUCK.

4 April 2009

THE G20 DEMONSTRATIONS IN LONDON... THE PLANNED APRIL 6TH STRIKES IN EGYPT...
HAS FIGHTING CAPITALISM BECOME FASHIONABLE NOW?

OMAR, MAY I REMIND YOU THAT CAPITALISM IS TO BLAME FOR THIS GLOBAL ECONOMIC CRISIS?!
NOT CAPITALISM, NADA. GREED.

GREED... BY THOSE WHO WANTED BIGGER HOMES FOR THEIR WIVES, NICER CLOTHES FOR THEIR CHILDREN AND KEPT ON WANTING MORE AND MORE AT THE EXPENSE OF HARD-WORKING VICTIMS!

SO YOU DO BLAME THE BANKERS!
NO, I BLAME THE POOR!

6 April 2009

BROTHERS AND SISTERS, THE MUSLIM BROTHERHOOD ARE PARTICIPATING TODAY IN **OUR** ANNIVERSARY OF THE APRIL 6TH STRIKE AND I SHALL HAVE NO PART OF THIS FAKE TRUCE!

THE UNITED WITH YASSER YOUSRY

BECAUSE FIFTY YEARS FROM NOW THEY'LL SAY IT WAS **THEIR** REVOLUTION!
JUST LIKE THEY DID TO NASSER!

THE UNITED WITH YASSER YOUSRY

WELL, I SAY THE MUSLIM BROTHERHOOD HAVE NO CLAIM TO DIVINITY!
IN FACT, I KNOW IN MY HEART THAT THE ALL-MERCIFUL HAS NOT FORGIVEN THEM FOR THEIR PAST SINS!

THE UNITED WITH ...SSER YOUSRY

AND NEITHER HAS GOD!
...E UNITED ...ITH ...ER YOUSRY

7 April 2009

YOUR EMINENCE, I'VE ALWAYS DEEMED BAHAIS AS INFIDELS, BUT IS BURNING THEIR HOMES JUSTIFIABLE?
OF COURSE NOT!!!

EXCEPT IF THEY BECOME A THREAT TO THE MORALITY OF SOCIETY...

WHAT IF THEY START SPREADING THEIR BELIEFS AMONG OUR INNOCENT CHILDREN?

... AND THEN BECOME SO LARGE AND POWERFUL THAT THEY BECOME INTOLERANT OF RELIGIOUS MINORITIES...

8 April 2009

OMAR, I'M RATHER DISTRAUGHT OVER LOSING MY JOB! I'M CONSIDERING A VACATION TO REDISCOVER MYSELF.
JANE, COME TO CAIRO! I MISS YOU! AND THE WEATHER IS GREAT!

EGYPT?! WELL... ARE THE PEOPLE THERE AS FRIENDLY AS I HEAR THEY ARE?
YES!

IS THE FOOD THERE AS YUMMY AS I HEAR IT IS?
YES!!

ARE THE PYRAMIDS AS MAGNIFICENT IN REAL LIFE AS THEY ARE IN THE BROCHURE?
THE WEATHER IS GREAT!

9 April 2009

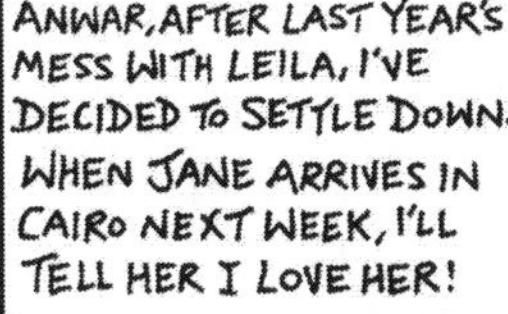
ANWAR, AFTER LAST YEAR'S MESS WITH LEILA, I'VE DECIDED TO SETTLE DOWN. WHEN JANE ARRIVES IN CAIRO NEXT WEEK, I'LL TELL HER I LOVE HER!

OMAR, IS THIS JUST SOME FOREIGN BLONDE FANTASY? OR IS SHE THE ONE YOU TRUST TO RAISE YOUR KIDS TO BE RELIGIOUS MEN?

DON'T WORRY. I'M SURE WHEN THE TIME COMES, JANE WILL RAISE OUR KIDS TO BE RATIONAL PEOPLE.

WHAT'S THE DIFFERENCE BETWEEN RELIGIOUS AND RATIONAL?!
THE NUMBER OF WIVES.

14 April 2009

LONDON: 2007
MY LOVELY JANE AND I ARE BUYING YOU ALL DRINKS TO CELEBRATE ANOTHER GREAT YEAR! MAY THE MARKETS STAY STRONG FOREVER!!

CHEERS, OMAR!!

CAIRO: TWO YEARS LATER
SO YOU'RE SAYING THE BANKERS ARE NO LONGER GETTING BIG BONUSES BECAUSE OF THE FINANCIAL CRISIS?
OMAR, THEY REMOVED THE WORD "BONUS" FROM THE DICTIONARY!

WOW! WHAT OTHER WORDS DID THEY REMOVE?
"AMBITION." "MORE." "FORECASTS." "LOBSTER." ....

WHAT'S LEFT?
"LEFT."

16 April 2009

THEY CAUGHT A FEW MEN OPERATING A LOCAL CELL FOR HEZBOLLAH IN EGYPT!
I THINK THE POLICE ARE TORTURING THEM BY NOW!! I KNOW HOW SAVAGE THEY CAN BE!!
BUT ANWAR...
VILE, SAVAGE, BRUTAL, INHUMAN THUG PUPPETS!! THEY HAVE NO RIGHT TO VIOLATE PEOPLE LIKE THAT!
BUT YOU MUST UNDERSTAND THE THREAT...
DAMN SAVAGE SHIITES!!
SORRY, BROTHER LEVY. WERE YOU TRYING TO SAY SOMETHING?
NO, MATE. YOU'RE DOING FINE!
© 2009. Tarek Shahin. www.alkhancomics.com

17 April 2009

PREVIOUSLY ON 'AL KHAN'...
BASMA, YOU WERE THE VICTIM OF A STREET ASSAULT!
WHY WON'T YOU TALK ABOUT IT?
WHAT ASSAULT?
NADA, YOUR SISTER HASN'T LEFT HER ROOM IN WEEKS!
IS SOMETHING WRONG?
BASMA WILL TALK TO YOU ABOUT... IT WHEN SHE'S READY, MAMA.
I HAVE THE PERFECT NEWS TO GET HER OUT OF THIS MOOD! I WAS ABLE TO CAST HER IN MY NEW MOVIE... IN A LEADING ROLE PLAYING A RAPE VICTIM!
NOooooOoOO-OOOoOOO!!!
I THINK SHE'LL SAY NO.
© 2009. Tarek Shahin. www.alkhancomics.com

21 April 2009

SO HAS THE CREDIT CRUNCH AFFECTED YOUR OPERATIONS?
WE'RE SELF-FINANCED, AND OUR INVESTORS BELIEVE IN OUR PROSPECTS.
YOU MENTIONED NEW MARKETS, LIKE EGYPT.
OH YEAH! EGYPT IS A KEY TARGET!
WE EXPECT TO DO VERY WELL THERE.
YOU SEE, RECENT DECISIONS BY THE EGYPTIAN GOVERNMENT HAVE OPENED THE MARKET TO FOREIGN ENTRANTS...
AND WE THINK EGYPT HAS A YOUNG DEMOGRAPHIC, RECEPTIVE TO NEW OFFERINGS GIVEN THE GAP IN THE MARKET.
THANK YOU, SIR.
PLEASE!! CALL ME HASSAN.
© 2009. Tarek Shahin. www.alkhancomics.com

22 April 2009

YASSER, I **WILL** ESTABLISH A LINK BETWEEN YOUR 'PROJECT LOVE' AND THE NEW TEEN RAPISTS!
WHAT'S YOUR PROOF, NADA?

I'M STILL WORKING ON THAT. BUT I TOLD YOU IDLE HANDS ARE--
NO! WHAT'S YOUR PROOF THAT THESE CRIMES EVER HAPPENED?

IF ALL THOSE WOMEN WHO WERE ALLEGEDLY ASSAULTED ARE TOO AFRAID OF SOCIETY TO GO TO THE POLICE, THEN THIS IS ALL HEARSAY!! WHAT KIND OF JOURNALIST WOULD THAT MAKE YOU, NADA?

SO YOU'RE GOING TO HIDE BEHIND SOCIETY'S MISJUDGEMENT?!
YOU OFFEND ME! I'M A MEMBER OF PARLIAMENT AND A TV HOST! **I AM** SOCIETY'S MISJUDGEMENT!

23 April 2009

I WANTED PROJECT LOVE TO LIBERATE THE YOUTH FROM OUR CORRUPT EDUCATION SYSTEM. I NEVER IMAGINED IT WOULD LEAD TO THIS!
SHE'S SCARED TO TALK ABOUT IT.

I CAN USE MY INFLUENCE TO ENSURE HER ANONYMITY. NADA, GIVE ME THE DRESS YOUR SISTER WAS WEARING! HER ATTACKERS MUST HAVE LEFT EVIDENCE THE POLICE CAN FIND.
GLAD YOU'RE DOING THE RIGHT THING, MR. YASSER.

BROTHERS AND SISTERS, I'M SORRY I REFUTED RUMORS OF RISING SEXUAL HARASSMENT ON THE STREETS OF CAIRO. IN FACT, TODAY I'D LIKE TO BE CANDID ABOUT WHO I THINK IS TO BLAME!
THE UNITED WITH YASSER YOUSRY

ALLOW ME TO PRESENT A VERY REVEALING EXHIBIT A!

24 April 2009

HOW COULD I HAVE BEEN SO STUPID?!!
NADA, LISTEN TO ME...

I LET YASSER YOUSRY FOOL ME INTO HELPING HIM BLAME THE WOMEN FOR BEING SEXUALLY ASSAULTED! I'M STUPID, BIG FALAFEL!

YOUSRY IS ONLY TELLING HIS FOLLOWERS WHAT THEY WANT TO HEAR! IT'S A CHEAP WAY OF GETTING PEOPLE TO LISTEN. NADA, YOU HEARING ME?

I'M STUPID! I'M STUPID! I'M STUPID! I'M STUPID!
YOU'RE STUPID! YOU'RE STUPID! YOU'RE STUPID! YOU'RE STUPID!

25 April 2009

I'M TELLING YOU, OMAR... MY COLLEAGUES IN THE GYNAECOLOGY DEPARTMENT ARE PERFORMING BACK DOOR OPERATIONS TO RECONSTRUCT WOMEN'S HYMENS!

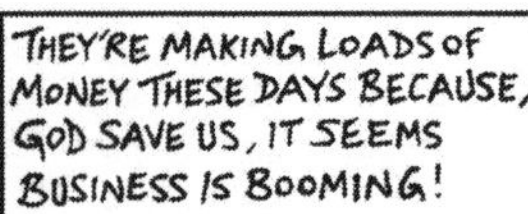
THEY'RE MAKING LOADS OF MONEY THESE DAYS BECAUSE, GOD SAVE US, IT SEEMS BUSINESS IS BOOMING!

EGYPTIAN WOMEN ARE FINALLY REALIZING THAT LOVE IS A GREATER VIRTUE THAN VIRGINITY?

OH, NO, NO, NO!! NOTHING DREADFUL LIKE THAT!!
NO, IT'S BOOMING BECAUSE RAPE IS ON THE RISE.

30 April 2009

SEE, SON? THIS SWINE FLU OUTBREAK IS GOD PUNISHING PORK EATERS!
BUT, BABA, WHAT ABOUT BIRD FLU?
SWINE FLU

NO, THAT WAS A TEST! GOD TESTS THE GOOD PEOPLE.
HOW DO WE KNOW IF WE'RE THE GOOD PEOPLE?

BY ASKING THOSE CLOSE TO US.
OH, GREAT! MAMA SAYS YOU'RE A GOOD HUSBAND!

SHE SAID THAT?
WELL, SHE SAID YOU WERE A TEST.

4 May 2009

YOUR EXCELLENCY, YOU CAN'T SLAUGHTER THE PIGS IN OUR FARM.
THE MINISTRY OF PROSPERITY APPRECIATES YOUR COOPERATION.

THIS IS MY LIVELIHOOD.
WE'RE PROTECTING THE LIVES OF MILLIONS OF EGYPTIANS!

BUT WHY KILL EVERY PIG IN THE COUNTRY?
THAT'S HOW WE'LL PREVENT THE SPREAD OF THE SWINE FLU.

HA HA HA
HA HA HA
HA HA HA

9 May 2009

YA LAHWY! YA LAHWY! GOD HELP US!!
MADAM, IS IT TRUE THE GOVERNMENT REDUCED THE SOCIAL WAGE RAISE FROM 30% TO ONLY 5%?
THOSE CANNIBALS!! THAT MEANS THAT IF YOU HAVE FIVE POUNDS NOW THAT WILL ONLY INCREASE BY 25 PIASTERS! YOU CAN'T EVEN BUY ENOUGH BREAD!!
WHY, GOD? WHY?
IN FACT, IF YOU HAVE FIVE POUNDS ON YOU, YOU MIGHT AS WELL JUST THROW IT AWAY TO AN OLD MAN LIKE ME, BECAUSE YOU CERTAINLY CAN'T FEED YOUR KIDS WITH ONLY FIVE POUNDS!
THANK YOU, MADAM, YOU'RE VERY KIND.
WHY?! WHY HAS THE GOVERNMENT ABANDONED THE MIDDLE CLASS?
THEY CALL IT THE "TRICKLE DOWN EFFECT." THOSE CANNIBALS!!

11 May 2009

MONA, WHAT'S THIS I HEAR ABOUT OMAR MARRYING SOME KHAWAGA GIRL FROM EUROPE?
JANE AND OMAR WERE IN LOVE WHEN HE WORKED IN LONDON.
THERE ARE PLENTY OF GOOD EGYPTIAN GIRLS. WHAT'S WRONG WITH YASMINE, MY DAUGHTER?
SOHA! THEY'RE COUSINS! IT'S NOT HEALTHY!
IT WAS COMMON IN OUR TIME! IN FACT, YASMINE'S OLDER SISTER MARRIED FROM WITHIN THE FAMILY AND THEY NOW HAVE A BEAUTIFUL BABY BOY!
OH, HOW'S THE BABY DOING? DID THE DOCTORS MANAGE TO FIX HIS BAD EYE?
NO, BUT THEY SAID HE'LL BE ABLE TO SEE WITH THE OTHER TWO!

13 May 2009

FACE IT, OMAR! YOU HURT THAT GIRL WHEN YOU LEFT HER! SHE'LL NEVER TAKE YOU BACK!
DON'T SAY THAT, ANWAR! YOU DON'T KNOW JANE!
YOU CAN'T MEND A BROKEN HEART. IT'S A PROVEN FACT OF LIFE! LIKE DEATH. LIKE TAXES. LIKE GOD.
HOLD ON! THAT ONE IS NOT A PROVEN FACT!!
EVERYBODY KNOWS TAXES ARE SUBJECT TO FISCAL POLICY.

14 May 2009

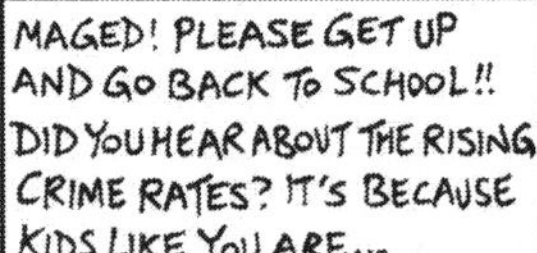

MAGED! PLEASE GET UP AND GO BACK TO SCHOOL!! DID YOU HEAR ABOUT THE RISING CRIME RATES? IT'S BECAUSE KIDS LIKE YOU ARE...

MR. YOUSRY SAID ON TV THAT EGYPTIAN WOMEN SHOULD COVER THEMSELVES UP IF THEY DON'T WANT TO BE ATTACKED. THOSE WOMEN HAD IT COMING!

I THINK MY LITTLE BROTHER MAGED MAY BE INVOLVED WITH THE NEW TEEN CRIME GANGS!

YA LAHWY!! INVOLVED?! AS IN WHAT CAPACITY?!
AS IN HEAD STRATEGIST AND CHIEF RAPIST.

15 May 2009

WE ASKED SOME MEMBERS OF THE COMMUNITY WHAT THEY THOUGHT OF THE RECENT EGYPTIAN COURT ORDER TO BAN PORN SITES.

TAKE A LOOK AT ALL THE YOUNG MEN WHO CAN'T AFFORD TO MARRY AND CAN'T TOUCH A WOMAN OUTSIDE OF MARRIAGE BECAUSE IT'S A SIN.

I HATE TO SAY THIS, BUT SOMETIMES PORN SITES ARE A LAST RESORT!
BANNING THEM WILL BE TORTURE!

YOU'RE SAYING THE GOVERNMENT IS ADDING TO THE MEN'S SENSE OF DEPRIVATION!
YEAH, OF COURSE.
THE MEN TOO.

16 May 2009

BABA, I'M AFRAID MAGED IS FALLING DOWN A DARK PATH! I CAN'T SAVE HIM.

I SPENT MY WHOLE LIFE TRYING TO BE LIKE YOU!
HE DOESN'T LOOK UP TO ME THE SAME WAY.

I'VE MADE MAGED FEEL INTELLECTUALLY INFERIOR.
I'VE MADE HIM THINK HE NEEDS TO CLIMB ENORMOUS MOUNTAINS IN ORDER TO BECOME HALF THE MAN I AM.

WHAT AM I DOING WRONG?

18 May 2009

OMAR, YOU REALLY THINK YOUR BROTHER HURT THOSE WOMEN?!
OF COURSE NOT!! BUT HE'S GOING DOWN THAT PATH! HE REFUSES TO GO TO SCHOOL!
THE PROPHET TOLD HIS FOLLOWERS TO SEEK EDUCATION! THAT'S YOUR PROBLEM, OMAR! YOU HAVEN'T BEEN TEACHING HIM ABOUT INSPIRATIONAL ROLE MODELS!
GIVE YOUR BROTHER TO ME FOR A FEW DAYS! LET'S PRAY THAT I CAN SUCCEED WHERE YOU HAVEN'T!
I'M RAISING MAGED JUST FINE, ANWAR! I ONLY NEED MORE TIME!
MORE TIME? GOD IS AVAILABLE TO LISTEN RIGHT NOW!
ALRIGHT! ALRIGHT! FINE! JUST... DON'T TELL HIM I'M HERE!
© 2009. Tarek Shahin. www.alkhancomics.com

20 May 2009

SO WHAT IF I DON'T HAVE PROOF AGAINST YOUSRY? WE'LL RUN A STORY SUGGESTING A POSSIBLE LINK BETWEEN HIS 'PROJECT LOVE' AND THE RISING CRIME RATE!
NO, IT WOULD NOT BE HEARSAY! WHO CARES WHAT OMAR WILL THINK?! HE'S NOT THE EDITOR! I AM! NO, I AM NOT TAKING THIS STORY TOO PERSONALLY! SHUT UP!!
I MISS YUNAN.
© 2009. Tarek Shahin. www.alkhancomics.com

21 May 2009

AAAAAH! OMAR, HELP ME! MY TUMMY!
MISS! MISS? ARE YOU ALRIGHT?
MISS? ARE YOU A TOURIST? WHO'S YOUR AGENT? YOU THINK SHE HAS THAT SWINE FLU?
NO, MAN! IT LOOKS LIKE FOOD POISONING!
THE HOSPITAL'S TOO FAR AWAY! LET'S TAKE HER TO THE LOCAL PHARMACY. THEY'LL GIVE HER PILLS OR SOMETHING!
CHECK HER POCKETS TO SEE IF SHE HAS MONEY TO PAY FOR THE PILLS!
I THOUGHT EGYPTIAN CHIVALRY WOULD ENDURE THE AGES!
IT HAS! THROUGH COST CUTTING!
© 2009. Tarek Shahin. www.alkhancomics.com

23 May 2009

OBAMA CHOSE EGYPT AS A VENUE FROM WHICH TO ADDRESS THE MUSLIM WORLD. WHY EGYPT?!
WELL, ANWAR, YOU DO HAVE THE AZHAR MOSQUE AND ALL.
OBAMA TO VISIT EGYPT
TRUE, BROTHER LEVY, BUT EGYPT HAS SINCE LOST ITS STATUS AS A ROLE MODEL WHEN IT ALLOWED ALCOHOL, BELLYDANCING AND INTEREST-BASED LENDING!
I LOVE MY COUNTRY BUT I JUST THINK THERE ARE OTHER, MORE SIGNIFICANT NATIONS IN THE MIDDLE EAST THAT HAVE PRESERVED THE RELIGIOUS IDENTITY!
YOU WANT OBAMA TO ADDRESS THE MUSLIM WORLD FROM ISRAEL?
OBAMA TO VISIT EGYPT

25 May 2009

AND SO THE MEMBERS OF THE UMMA MUST WORK HARD, BUT KNOW THAT YOUR ACHIEVEMENTS ARE ALL PREORDAINED!
MMMM... LISTEN, MAGED! GOOD WORDS. GOOD WORDS.
DR. ANWAR, I DON'T UNDERSTAND A SINGLE WORD THIS MAN IS SAYING! DO YOU?
NOT ENTIRELY.
WELL, IF YOU DON'T UNDERSTAND IT, HOW DO YOU KNOW IT'S GOOD?
HOW DO YOU KNOW IT'S NOT?

28 May 2009

JANE, I'M SO SORRY! MY BROTHER NEEDED MY HELP. I DIDN'T KNOW YOU FELL ILL! I PROMISE I'LL NEVER LEAVE YOU AGAIN!
OMAR, WAIT! I NEED TO TELL YOU SOMETHING. I'VE... FALLEN IN LOVE WITH SOMEONE!
ME?
SOMEONE ELSE I'VE ONLY RECENTLY MET!
MYSELF?
HIS NAME IS YUNAN.
I?

30 May 2009

DR. ATEF, MY GRANDSON FINISHED A COURSE OF VITAMINS. YOU SURE HE NEEDS MORE?
THE MORE THE MERRIER! I'VE BEEN GIVING THEM TO MY SON YUNAN ALL HIS LIFE!
DR. ATEF SALIB PHARMACY
HOW IS YUNAN? I HAVEN'T SEEN HIM SINCE HE WAS A LITTLE BOY.
DOING GREAT! HE WAS A PHOTOGRAPHER WITH SOME MAGAZINE. BUT NOW HE HAS A REAL, MORE SECURE JOB!
THAT'LL BE 98 POUNDS.
HERE'S 100.
DR. ATEF SALIB PHARMACY
YUNAN... WHAT DO WE SAY TO THE NICE LADY?
"SORRY, MADAM. I SWEAR TO GOD I DON'T HAVE ANY CHANGE."
CASHIER

1 June 2009

OMAR!! OH MY GOD! IT'S SO GOOD TO SEE YO...
JUDAS!! I LOVE HER, MAN!!
WELL... I RESPECT HER!! I RESPECT YOU BOTH! BUT YOU CAN'T POSSIBLY THINK THAT SOMEONE LIKE HER WOULD EVER WANT TO BE WITH SOMEONE LIKE YOU! HONESTY IS NOT TREACHERY!
YUNAN, HOW DARE YOU? YOU DON'T KNOW JANE LIKE I DO!
I'VE KNOWN NADA A LOT LONGER THAN YOU HAVE!
WHAT?
WHO?

2 June 2009

..ONE WEEK EARLIER...
SO THOSE TWO MEN CARRIED ME AND THEN I WOKE UP IN YOUR FATHER'S PHARMACY?
HE'S CALLING IN A DOCTOR. MY NAME IS YUNAN. ARE YOU A TOURIST?
HOW ARE YOU FEELING NOW, YOUNG LADY? I'M NOT ACTUALLY A PHARMACIST BUT YOU EITHER HAVE FOOD POISONING OR IF I'M RIGHT IT'S JUST...
I DON'T RECALL THE LAST TIME A MAN ASKED ME HOW I WAS FEELING! MY HEART IS POUNDING!
REALLY? YOUR HEART IS POUNDING?
THEN I AM RIGHT! BABA! IT'S JUST GAS!

3 June 2009

So THAT WOMAN WAS JANE? YOUR JANE?! OMAR, I HAD NO IDEA! I WOULD NEVER...
I KNOW, YUNAN. OF COURSE I BELIEVE YOU.
BESIDES, YOU'RE GETTING MARRIED NEXT MONTH ANYWAY!
...TO A WOMAN I DON'T LOVE, PRESSURED BY MY PARENTS.
SO THE QUESTION IS, SHOULD I RESPOND TO THE FEELINGS OF THIS NEW WOMAN WHO GENUINELY LOVES ME?
AND YOU'RE PROBABLY THINKING, WHY WOULD JANE WANT YOU WHEN SHE CAN HAVE ME?
OR SHOULD I CHOOSE MY FRIENDSHIP WITH A SELF-OBSESSED, CONDESCENDING MAN?
F#@?!! THERE'S A THIRD GUY?!

6 June 2009

HE PRAISED PROPHET MUHAMMAD! HE QUOTED THE QURAN!
ALLAH AKBAR! OBAMA!! OBAMA!!!
AND BEFORE THAT IN SAUDI ARABIA HE SAID "SHOUKRAN" IN ARABIC!
WELCOME OBAMA, FRIEND OF ISLAM!
WAIT! WHEN HE THANKED THE SAUDI KING, DID OBAMA SAY IT WITH A "B" OR A "P"?
BETROL! HE SAID "BETROL" IN ARABIC!
WELCOME OBAMA, FRIEND OF ISLAM!

8 June 2009

BASMA, YOU HAVEN'T LEFT YOUR ROOM SINCE YOU WERE ASSAULTED! COME ON, I KNOW YOU'RE BRAVER THAN THAT.
NADA, YOU THINK I SHOULD COVER MY HEAD WITH THIS SCARF?
ABSOLUTELY NOT!
IF YOU WANT TO WEAR THE HIJAB, I'LL RESPECT THAT, AS LONG AS IT'S NOT OF A FEAR OF SOCIETY BUT A CHOICE THAT YOU MAKE.
YOU'RE RIGHT. I HAVE MADE MY CHOICE. I'LL GO WITH THE PRADA SCARF INSTEAD.

9 June 2009

YUNAN, YOU WOULDN'T BE BETRAYING OMAR! HE LEFT ME A LONG TIME AGO!
I FELL IN LOVE WITH YOU!
YOUR PARENTS MADE YOU LEAVE YOUR JOB AS A PHOTOGRAPHER BECAUSE IT WASN'T GOOD ENOUGH FOR A BRIDE THEY CHOSE FOR YOU!
BE WITH ME AND YOU'LL ESCAPE THE CLUTCHES OF EGYPTIAN SOCIETY!
YES... OH YES, SWEET FREEDOM!
SUPERB! NOW YOU MUST TELL YOUR PARENTS THE NEWS.
WHAT?! YOU WANT MY PARENTS TO FIND OUT I'M STANDING UP TO THEM?

10 June 2009

PROJECT LOVE WAS A WASTE OF TIME! I ONLY HAVE DAYS TO STUDY FOR MY EXAMS!
MAGED, THAT'S GREAT! I'M SURPRISED IT WAS ANWAR WHO INSPIRED YOU.
PHYSICS
DR. ANWAR WORKS HARD FOR HIS FAMILY AND HE ALSO TREATS POOR PATIENTS FOR FREE.
OMAR, WHY DO YOU ALWAYS MAKE FUN OF HIM AND CALL HIM BACKWARD MINDED?
I NEVER SAID HE WAS A BAD PERSON... JUST NOT MY INTELLECTUAL IDOL!
PHYSICS
SPEAKING OF YOUR IDOL, I'VE BEEN MEANING TO ASK YOU... WHO IS JOHN GALT?
I'M NOT SURE ANYMORE.

15 June 2009

OMAR, IF THE SWINE FLU HAS REACHED EGYPT, WHY DON'T YOU JUST BUY MY FATHER'S PHARMACY?
STOP IT, YUNAN! I'M NOT THAT KIND OF INVESTOR!
MILLIONS OF EGYPTIANS WILL WANT SURGICAL MASKS AND FLU SHOTS!
IT'S WRONG TO PROFIT THAT WAY! THAT'S NOT WHO I AM!
I DON'T BELIEVE YOU, OMAR!
TENS OF MILLIONS OF EGYPTIANS CAN'T AFFORD TO GO TO THE PHARMACY! THEY MAY RESORT TO ALTERNATIVE MEDICINE.
YOU MEAN DRINKING CAMEL URINE?!
I'M A MASS MARKET INVESTOR!
OMAR'S BOOL AID INC. ☎ 1-900-PISS

18 June 2009

YUNAN, WE ALREADY PROMISED GERGES YOU'D MARRY HIS DAUGHTER MARIAN!
NOW YOU TELL ME YOU'VE FALLEN IN LOVE WITH SOME TOURIST FROM ENGLAND?
THIS IS CATASTROPHIC. BUT AT LEAST YOU DIDN'T COMPLICATE THINGS MORE BY FALLING IN LOVE WITH A MUSLIM GIRL!
JANE IS BUDDHIST.
YOUR WIFE'S COMA COULD LAST UP TO TWO WEEKS. WE'LL KEEP MONITORING HER.
YUNAN, DID YOU SAY SOMETHING TO UPSET YOUR MOTHER?
EMERGENCY ROOM
YOUR FATHER'S COMA COU…
THANKS DOCTOR. I GET IT.
EMERGENCY ROOM

19 June 2009

IRAN
WHERE IS MY VOTE?
EUROPE
WHERE IS MY EQUALITY?
AMERICA
WHERE IS MY DREAM?
EGYPT
WHERE IS MY REPLAY?
BRAZIL SCORED AN UNFAIR PENALTY!!

20 June 2009

YOUR EXCELLENCY, THE IRANIAN FOOTBALL TEAM HAS WORN GREEN BANDS IN SOLIDARITY WITH IRAN'S OPPOSITION!
OH MY GOD! WHAT IF EGYPT'S FOOTBALL TEAM DOES THE SAME?!
IT COULD HAVE UNCONTROLLABLE CONSEQUENCES!
THAT'S IT! THE MINISTRY OF PROSPERITY WILL START A CAMPAIGN TO MAKE FOOTBALL UNPOPULAR!
SIR! FOOTBALL IS THE PRIDE AND PASSION OF MILLIONS OF EGYPTIANS!
WOULDN'T IT BE EASIER FOR US TO MAKE THE PRESIDENT A LITTLE MORE POPULAR?!
FELLOW CITIZENS, THE NATIONAL RESEARCH AGENCY HAS FOUND A LINK BETWEEN FOOTBALL AND TESTICULAR CANCER.

22 June 2009

So Jane is Buddhist and you can't marry a non-Coptic!
And you can only marry from the people of the Book!
Sharia laws on inter-faith marriage have differing interpretations.
So Jane is mine!! Too bad you're not a Muslim, Yunan!
Oh, and, are you?!
My name is Omar Mohamed Adel Shukri!
So, relatively speaking...
© 2009. Tarek Shahin. www.alkhancomics.com

23 June 2009

Iran hated the term "Axis of Evil" and now the regime is labelling the unarmed protesters as "terrorists!"
They accused the world media of covering up inaccuracies in the Holocaust and now they're blocking media coverage of the post-election riots!
Omar, I never thought the world would ever see a pro-Arabist regime become so oppressive!
It's shocking, Nada!
That the Iranian regime would disappoint like this?
No, that you've never heard of Nasser!
© 2009. Tarek Shahin. www.alkhancomics.com

24 June 2009

Nada! Omar won't give me my job back because of this Jane thing!
Yunan! First you abruptly walk out of Alkhan to appease your parents.
And then I'm hit with a family tragedy and when I look around for my best friend, you're not there! Meanwhile, the region is destabilizing, Egypt is transitioning...
And now you come back to chat about your little feud, where all that's at stake is your love life and Omar's ego?!
Continue.
© 2009. Tarek Shahin. www.alkhancomics.com

25 June 2009

MAGED BARELY PASSED HIS EXAMS. HE MUST WORK HARDER NEXT YEAR.
YOUR LITTLE BROTHER IS A GOOD BOY, OMAR.
ANWAR, YOU'RE THE ONE WHO SAVED HIM! HOW CAN I THANK YOU? I'LL BUY YOU A KEBAB MEAL. I'LL ADD SOME KOFTA!
YOU CAN THANK ME BY SEEING TO IT THAT YOUR BROTHER REMAINS ON A RIGHTEOUS PATH, WHERE HIS DEEDS ARE MEANINGFUL BOTH ON EARTH AND IN ETERNITY.
THAT'S ALL?
ADD SOME HUMUS AND BABA GHANOUG.

29 June 2009*

30 June 2009

I'M BORED.
I'M HUNGRY.
LOOK OVER THERE! LUNCH!!
PSSSST! HEY PUSSY CAT! COME HERE!
COME ON, HOT STUFF! WHERE ARE YOU GOING?!
YOU KNOW YOU WANT IT!
I HATE IT WHEN THEY TEASE US.

Notes by the author:
* Michael Jackson, 1958 - 2009

1 July 2009

HELP!
COME ON, HOT STUFF! JUST ONE KISS!
EXCUSE ME, SON!
EXCUSE ME, SON! CAN YOU SPARE SOME CHANGE?
GO AWAY, OLD MAN. GET A JOB!
PLEASE! I KNOW YOU'RE LOADED! I CAN FEEL YOUR MONEY SACKS.
THAT'S... NOT MY MONEY SACK.
AAAAAHHHH!
I KNOW.

2 July 2009

BIG FALAFEL, YOU TOLD ME IF I WANTED TO SPEAK TO ONE OF THE SEXUAL HARASSMENT VICTIMS, I SHOULD ASK OMAR.
RIGHT.
WELL, I DID. HE HAD NO IDEA WHAT I WAS TALKING ABOUT!
DID YOU ASK HIM ABOUT THE WIFE OF HIS FRIEND ANWAR?
WHO'S ANWAR?!
I TOLD YOU TO---
NADA, WHAT EXACTLY DID YOU SAY TO OMAR?!
I BLAME YOUR HAIR. THERE'S STYLISH AND THEN THERE'S PRETTY!
HUH?!

4 July 2009

PREVIOUSLY ON 'AL KHAN'...
HELP!
COME ON, HOT STUFF! JUST ONE KISS!
STOP LYING, AISHA! YOU'RE SAYING TWO MEN HARASSED YOU IN THE STREET?!
I'M YOUR WIFE, ANWAR! I WOULDN'T LIE!
YOU'RE A FULLY VEILED WOMAN!! HAVE THE MEN IN THIS COUNTRY BECOME SO DESPERATE THEY WON'T SPARE THE PIOUS?!
I FEEL SO VIOLATED.
I'M SORRY THIS HAPPENED TO YOU, ANWAR.

7 July 2009*

NADA, HOW DO YOU KNOW ANWAR?
I DON'T. BUT MY SOURCE TELLS ME YOUR FRIEND'S WIFE WAS A VICTIM OF STREET HARASSMENT.
IMPOSSIBLE! ANWAR'S WIFE WEARS A NIQAB! A BURKA!
SHE'S FULLY VEILED?! EVEN BETTER! OMAR, I HAVE TO INTERVIEW HER FOR MY STORY!!
ARE YOU INSANE?! NADA, YOU DON'T UNDERSTAND! ANWAR KEEPS HER HIDDEN FROM SOCIETY! I'VE NEVER SEEN HER! SHE'S AS HIDDEN AS THE MYSTERIES OF THE PYRAMIDS, AS UNTRACEABLE AS THE HOLY GRAIL...
I DON'T CARE IF SHE'S AS INVISIBLE AS THE SPLIT IN THE NATIONAL DEMOCRATIC PARTY!!
FIND HER!!
© 2009. Tarek Shahin. www.alkhancomics.com

8 July 2009

NADA, IF YOU MUST INTERVIEW ANWAR'S WIFE ABOUT HER HARASSMENT INCIDENT CAN'T YOU DO IT BY PHONE?
NO, OMAR.
I NEED TO PUT HER FACE ON THE COVER OF ALKHAN SO READERS CAN FEEL HER ANGUISH!
SHE WEARS A FACE VEIL!! HOW WILL A PHOTO OF HER EYES TELL ANY STORY?!
ONLY IF TAKEN BY EGYPT'S MOST SKILLFUL PHOTOGRAPHER. THAT IS, IF YOU CAN RISE ABOVE YOUR FEUD!
YOU'RE RIGHT, NADA.
HEY, YUNAN!
YUNAN, DO YOU KNOW ANYONE?
GROW UP, OMAR. LET'S GO!
© 2009. Tarek Shahin. www.alkhancomics.com

9 July 2009**

OMAR, WE'RE ABOUT TO VISIT ANWAR'S WIFE TO INTERVIEW HER! MAKE SURE ANWAR DOESN'T COME BACK HOME!
9:12:24
I'LL KEEP HIM WITHIN MY EYE SIGHT AT ALL TIMES! GOOD LUCK, NADA!
AL KHAN
THE FOLLOWING TAKES PLACE BETWEEN AROUND 1:00 PM AND SOMETIME AFTER THE MAGHREB PRAYER INSHALLAH
HAMED, HAVE YOU SEEN ANWAR? WE WERE SUPPOSED TO MEET FOR A SHISHA!
DR. ANWAR WAS AT THE MOSQUE...
1:12:24
HE RAN INTO SOME AZHAR STUDENTS FROM UZBEKISTAN. HE'S TEACHING THEM ARABIC.
NADA, WE HAVE A SOVIET SITUATION! ABORT! ABORT!
© 2009. Tarek Shahin. www.alkhancomics.com

Notes by the author:

* Younger leaders of the authoritarian NDP had claimed a split with its old guard.

** "Inshalaa" means "God willing." This was a spoof of US television drama "24."

10 July 2009

WE CAN'T JUST BARGE INTO THE HOME OF A WOMAN WE'VE NEVER MET AND ASK HER ABOUT BEING HARASSED! SHE'LL FREAK OUT, NADA!
YUNAN, EGYPTIAN WOMEN ARE INCREASINGLY FALLING VICTIM TO SEXUAL HARASSMENT ON THE STREETS AND NONE OF THEM ARE TALKING ABOUT IT! AS JOURNALISTS, WE MUST BRING THE ISSUE TO LIGHT!
WHAT IF SHE REFUSES TO BE INTER-VIEWED?
PLEASE! I'VE INTERVIEWED UNION LEADERS, PRO-DEMOCRACY BLOGGERS, MINISTERS...
NONE OF THESE PEOPLE WERE SEXUALLY ASSAULTED.
I INTERVIEWED THOSE BLOGGERS AFTER THEY WERE ARRESTED.
© 2009. Tarek Shahin. www.alkhancomics.com

11 July 2009

I NOTICED YOU DIDN'T WRITE ABOUT THE HIJAB MARTYR.
WE REPORTED ON THE MURDER.
YES, BUT YOU DIDN'T EXPOSE THE SPREAD OF ISLAMOPHOBIA IN EUROPE!
I'M HOPING THIS WILL TURN OUT TO BE A ONE-OFF INCIDENT.
SINCE 9/11, OVER NEARLY A TEN YEAR SPAN, THOSE INFIDELS HAVE BEEN PERSECUTING AND ATTACKING MUSLIMS EVERY DAY!! AND YOU SAY THIS MAY HAVE BEEN A ONE-OFF INCIDENT?
NO, I'M HOPING IN A TEN MILLION YEAR HORIZON, THIS PLANET WILL TURN OUT TO BE A ONE-OFF INCIDENT.
AL KHAN
© 2009. Tarek Shahin. www.alkhancomics.com

13 July 2009*

MY NAME'S NADA. WE'RE FROM AL KHAN MAGAZINE. ARE YOU AISHA?
WHAT DO YOU WANT? I'M NOT ALLOWED TO LET ANYONE IN!!
LAST WEEK YOU WERE SEXUALLY HARASSED ON THE STREET, CORRECT?
NO! INCORRECT! MY HUSBAND ANWAR WOULD KILL ME IF I SPOKE TO REPORTERS!
WE'LL CITE YOU ANONYMOUSLY. THINK HOW MANY WOMEN YOU'LL INSPIRE IF YOU TALK!
BRAVO, AISHA! BEFORE WE BEGIN, DO YOU NEED A HUG?
I NEED A DRINK.
© 2009. Tarek Shahin. www.alkhancomics.com

Notes by the author:

* This strip caused fury. I think it was misunderstood.

14 July 2009

AISHA, I'M TRYING TO ESTABLISH A LINK BETWEEN THE SCHOOL BOYCOTT PROJECT HELMED BY MP YASSER YOUSRY AND THE RISING RATE OF CRIMES, LIKE SEXUAL HARASSMENT.
THOSE TWO GUYS WHO HARASSED YOU, WERE THEY STUDENTS WHO LOOKED LIKE THEY'D JOINED 'PROJECT LOVE?'
NADA, YOU'RE PUTTING WORDS IN HER MOUTH!
QUIET, YUNAN! I'M THE ONE CONDUCTING THE INTERVIEW!
STOP IT! YOU SOUND JUST LIKE THEM!!
THOSE TWO GUYS WERE FIGHTING OVER YOU, TOO?
NO. THEY, TOO, WANTED TO PUT THINGS IN MY MOUTH!

15 July 2009

AL KHAN MAGAZINE HAS RUN AN INTERVIEW WITH A FULLY VEILED FEMALE VICTIM OF SEXUAL HARASSMENT, IN AN ATTEMPT TO UNDERMINE MY YOUTH ANGER INITIATIVE.
AL KHAN
WELL, I STILL ASSERT THAT THE RULING REGIME HAS FUELED CORRUPTION AND CORPORATE EXCESS, AND DISENFRANCHISED OUR YOUTH. NOTHING BUT CRIME HAS TRICKLED DOWN TO THE STREETS OF EGYPT.
I'VE BEEN A MEMBER OF THE OPPOSITION FOR YEARS AND IT REMAINS MY DUTY TO REMEDY OUR GOVERNMENT'S FAILINGS BY BEING MEANINGFUL AND CONSTRUCTIVE.
THE UNITED WITH YASSER YOUSRY
IT'S NEVER TOO LATE FOR ME TO START.
THE UNITED WITH YASSER YOUSRY

16 July 2009

MR. YOUSRY, IF I CAN'T PROVE THAT 'PROJECT LOVE' LED TO MORE CRIME, CAN YOU LIVE WITH YOURSELF KNOWING THERE'S A 1% CHANCE IT MAY HAVE?
WHAT DO YOU SUGGEST, NADA?
INSTEAD OF TELLING KIDS TO BOYCOTT SCHOOL, USE YOUR POSITION IN PARLIAMENT TO SEEK AN OVERHAUL OF THE EDUCATION SYSTEM!
IF EGYPT'S EDUCATION SYSTEM IS OUTDATED AND MISGUIDING, WORK TO MAKE IT PROGRESSIVE AND ENCOMPASSING.
PROGRESSIVE. ENCOMPASSING. RIGHT.
WHAT ELSE CAN I DO?
LOTS! OLD MAN, THERE'S MORE TO SOCIALISM THAN JUST NONESENSE.

17 July 2009

YUNAN, SEEING YOU WORK FOR THE MAGAZINE AGAIN... I CAN'T LET JANE GET BETWEEN OUR FRIENDSHIP. TO ME SHE'S JUST A LAST LINK TO MY PREVIOUS LIFE.
OMAR, WE BOTH KNOW I DON'T LOVE HER EITHER. I ONLY SAW HER AS AN ESCAPE FROM MY FAMILY-ARRANGED MARRIAGE.
LOOKS LIKE WE'RE BOTH GOING TO BE SINGLE MEN IN CAIRO UNTIL WE DIE.
THE DIFFERENCE IS, YOU STILL HAVE YOUR YOUTH.
YOU'RE RIGHT. YOU'LL PROBABLY DIE BEFORE I DO.
HEY! DON'T HATE THE PLAYER, HATE THE GAME.

18 July 2009

BROTHERS AND SISTERS, YESTERDAY I MET WITH CABINET MEMBERS TO PROPOSE A JOINT EDUCATION REFORM INITIATIVE.
BUT THEN THEY TRIED TO TRICK ME!!
THE UNITED WITH YASSER YOUSRY
"WE CAN'T WORK WITH THE OPPOSITION," THEY SAID! THE NATIONAL DEMOCRATIC PARTY, OF COURSE, WANTS TO BELITTLE THE OPPOSITION BY TAKING MY IDEAS AND SELLING THEM TO THE PUBLIC AS THEIR OWN!
...BUT THE JOKE'S ON THEM! BECAUSE WHETHER THEY LIKE IT OR NOT, I WILL FIGHT FOR REFORM...
...FROM WITHIN! THIS MORNING I BECAME AN OFFICIAL MEMBER OF THE NATIONAL DEMOCRATIC PARTY! HOW DARE THEY UNDER-ESTIMATE THE OPPOSITION?!
THE ONE WITH YASSER YOUSRY

20 July 2009

MARIAN, FAMILY-ARRANGED MARRIAGES ARE LOVELESS! YOU CAN'T MARRY YUNAN JUST BECAUSE YOUR PARENTS SHOWED YOU HIS FACE IN A PHOTO ALBUM!
IS THAT WHAT THEY TOLD YOU?!
OMAR, I DIDN'T PICK HIM OUT OF A PHOTO ALBUM!! I'VE ALWAYS ADMIRED HIS WORK AS A PHOTOJOURNALIST, LONG BEFORE I MET HIM AND FOUND HIM TO BE THE SWEETEST GENTLEMAN.
YOU MEAN YOU ACTUALLY HAVE REAL FEELINGS FOR YUNAN?! WHY DIDN'T YOU SAY SOMETHING BEFORE?!!
HIS MOTHER SAID SILENCE WAS A SIGN OF APPROVAL!
HE THINKS YOU'RE A DULL, INANIMATE BORE!
HE DOES?! WAS IT SOMETHING I SAID?

22 July 2009

HOW COULD YOUSRY JOIN THE NDP?!! ...BETRAYING NASSER ON THE ANNIVERSARY OF HIS REVOLUTION!!
YOU SHOULD'VE SEEN IT COMING, NADA. THE NDP IS IN MANY WAYS AN EXTENSION OF NASSER'S RULE OF EGYPT.
HOW COULD YOU SAY THAT, BIG FALAFEL?! WHAT ABOUT ARAB UNITY AND WORKERS' RIGHTS?
NASSER HAD A NOBLE CAUSE! WHAT DOES THE NDP HAVE?!
HIS PRISONS.

28 July 2009

SO, MARIAN, IS IT TRUE YOU'RE STUDYING PHOTOGRAPHY?
YES. I NOW UNDERSTAND FOCAL RATIO.
YUNAN, I REALLY ADMIRED YOUR PHOTO ESSAYS ON IRAQ AND THE EGYPT FOOD RIOTS.
MARIAN, ADMIRATION AND LOVE ARE TWO DIFFERENT THINGS.
WELL, IN THAT CASE, I HOPE TO ONE DAY FIND SOMEONE AS ARTICULATE AND SWEET AS YOU...
MARIAN, SHUT UP!!
YOU HAD ME AT FOCAL RATIO.

29 July 2009

AL KHAN
JULY 2009
SPECIAL REPORT "I WAS SEXUALLY HARASSED ON THE STREETS OF CAIRO"
AL KHAN
OMAR, YOU CONNIVING... YOU INTERVIEWED MY WIFE WITHOUT MY PERMISSION?!
ANWAR, THE WOMAN IN THE MAGAZINE IS FULLY VEILED! HOW DO YOU KNOW IT'S YOUR...
AL KHAN
YOU DIDN'T THINK I'D RECOGNIZE THE TEARS OF THE WOMAN WHO SHARES MY BED?!!

31 July 2009

MARIAN, WHERE HAVE YOU BEEN ALL MY LIFE? WILL YOU MARRY ME?
YUNAN, ACCORDING TO OUR PARENTS, WE'RE ALREADY ENGAGED!
MARIAN. WILL YOU MARRY ME?
GOOD QUESTION.
YES!
LOLOLOLOLO-LOLOLOLOLO-LOYYYY!!!
© 2009. Tarek Shahin. www.alkhancomics.com

1 August 2009

BABA, MARIAN AND I ARE GETTING MARRIED, BUT IT'S BECAUSE WE'VE FALLEN IN LOVE, NOT BECAUSE YOU THINK WE SHOULD!
YUNAN, WE NEVER MEANT TO FORCE YOU INTO THIS MARRIAGE. WE WERE JUST WORRIED YOU'D GROW OLD WITHOUT FINDING A GOOD EGYPTIAN GIRL WITH WHOM TO SHARE YOUR LIFE.
SO DO WE HAVE YOUR BLESSING?
MAY THIS UNION BE BLESSED WITH HEALTH AND HAPPINESS...
...AND MAY YOUR FIRST CHILD BE AN AMERICAN AND/OR CANADIAN CHILD.
© 2009. Tarek Shahin. www.alkhancomics.com

3 August 2009

YUNAN ASKED MARIAN TO MARRY HIM. SO WHERE DOES THAT LEAVE US, JANE?
OMAR, I THINK I'VE OUTSTAYED MY WELCOME IN CAIRO.
JANE, I ONLY LEFT YOU BECAUSE I HAD TO LEAVE LONDON. MY FAMILY NEEDED ME.
AND THAT'S WHY I'LL ALWAYS LOVE YOU. GOOD BYE, OMAR.
IF YOU LEAVE ME I'LL HAVE NO REASON TO LIVE!
DARLING, THERE ARE 17 MILLION PEOPLE IN CAIRO! AND FROM WHAT I'VE EXPERIENCED...
...THAT'S 17 MILLION REASONS TO WAKE UP EVERY MORNING!
© 2009. Tarek Shahin. www.alkhancomics.com

5 August 2009

EGYPT'S FORMER MUFTI SAYS EXPORTING GAS TO ISRAEL IS 'HARAM.' A SIN!
MUFTI SAYS

EGYPT SHOULD SEPARATE RELIGION AND THE STATE.
I TOTALLY AGREE, LEVY.
MUFTI SAYS

IF THE ARABS CONTINUE TO LET MULLAHS AND SHEIKHS DICTATE POLICY, THEY WILL NEVER MAKE PROGRESS IN THEIR PEACE WITH ISRAEL.

BECAUSE ISRAEL SEPARATES RELIGION AND THE JEWISH STATE?
MUFTI SAYS

8 August 2009

Letters to the Editor

"Dear Al Khan,
I feel your interview with the sexual harassment victim last week contained some unnecessary graphic details and may have tarnished Egypt's image."

Dear reader,
Thank you for your letter. While we appreciate your concerns, Al Khan is committed to the truth.

Nada Saleh,
Chief Editor, Al Khan

Letters to the Editor

"Dear Al Khan,
Your profile of parliament member Yasser Yousry was clearly biased, perhaps even influenced by your publisher Mr. Omar."

Dear reader,
Thank you for your letter. I assure you, the editors have full editorial control and excercise objectivity.

Nada Saleh,
Chief Editor, Al Khan

Letters to the Editor

"Dear Al Khan,
I think the ongoing animosity between Omar and Nada will eventually turn into love and they'll end up together."

Dear reader,
Thank you for your letter. But, no.

Nada Saleh,
Chief Editor, Al Khan

Letters to the Editor

"Dear Al Khan,
Is it because Nada is a poor judge of character or is it because she feels inadequate?"

Dear reader,
I recognize your email address, Omar. Stop sending letters to the editor every time you get stuck in a traffic jam.

Nada Saleh,
Chief Editor, Al Khan

10 August 2009

IN THE NAME OF OUR LORD.... WE DECLARE THE MARRIAGE OF THE BLESSED ORTHODOX SON YUNAN TO THE BLESSED ORTHODOX DAUGHTER MARIAN.

CAN YOU BELIEVE OUR SON IS FINALLY MARRIED?
FINALLY EMANCI-PATED. OFF TO THEIR NEW HOME.

...WELL, EVENTUALLY. I CAN'T BELIEVE THE TILE WORKERS AND CARPENTERS DIDN'T FINISH ON TIME!

DOES OUR SON KNOW HE'LL SPEND THE FIRST MONTHS OF MARRIED LIFE AT HIS PARENTS' HOME?
SHHHH! DON'T RUIN THE SURPRISE!!

12 August 2009

THE RULING PARTY IS HOLDING AN ONLINE "OPEN" DIALOGUE." THEY WANT YOUNG EGYPTIANS TO SEND QUESTIONS.

OMAR, CAN I ASK THEM ANYTHING I WANT?
YES, MAGED. I THINK THEY DO WANT TO ADDRESS PUBLIC MATTERS.

ANYTHING?!
SURE.

"WHAT IS EGYPT'S FUTURE?"
MAGED, NO! THAT'S A PRIVATE MATTER!

13 August 2009

...THE FISHERMEN THEN MANAGED TO OVERPOWER THE SOMALI PIRATES, WHO HAD TAKEN THEM CAPTIVE FOR FOUR MONTHS.
WE WERE, OF COURSE, MONITORING.

YOUR EXCELLENCY, WAS THIS AN ACT OF COURAGE BY THE FISHERMEN OR DID THE EGYPTIAN GOVERNMENT PLAY AN ACTUAL ROLE IN THEIR FREEDOM?

WELL, I COULD HAVE STOOD HERE AND TOUTED THE ROLE OF THE GOVERNMENT, BUT THAT WOULD HAVE ACCOMPLISHED NOTHING. WHAT YOU SHOULD HAVE ASKED IS WHETHER THE FISHERMEN ARE NOW SAFE!

"COULDA," "WOULDA," "SHOULDA".
THANKS.

14 August 2009

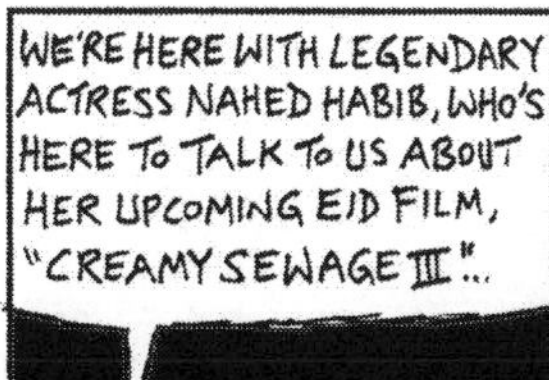
WE'RE HERE WITH LEGENDARY ACTRESS NAHED HABIB, WHO'S HERE TO TALK TO US ABOUT HER UPCOMING EID FILM, "CREAMY SEWAGE III"...

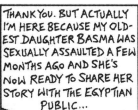

THANK YOU. BUT ACTUALLY I'M HERE BECAUSE MY OLDEST DAUGHTER BASMA WAS SEXUALLY ASSAULTED A FEW MONTHS AGO AND SHE'S NOW READY TO SHARE HER STORY WITH THE EGYPTIAN PUBLIC...

WOW, BASMA! WHO INSPIRED YOU TO DEFY THE SOCIAL STIGMA? WAS IT THE 'BRA-BURNING' FEMINISTS OF THE WEST?
WELL....

...AMONG OTHERS.
AL KHAN

18 August 2009

I'M STANDING IN FRONT OF THE WHITE HOUSE WHERE PRESIDENT OBAMA IS TO HOLD AN HISTORIC MEETING WITH HIS EGYPTIAN COUNTERPART.

DO YOU THINK ANY PROGRESS CAN BE MADE, GIVEN THE STRAINED RELATIONSHIP BEWTEEN THE TWO SIDES...?

...WON'T PAST PHRASES LIKE "TYRANT OF AFRICA" COME IN THE WAY?

GOOD QUESTION. BUT I'M SURE EGYPT WILL AGREE THAT THE U.S. REPUBLICANS SHOULD STOP CALLING MR. OBAMA SUCH NAMES.

19 August 2009

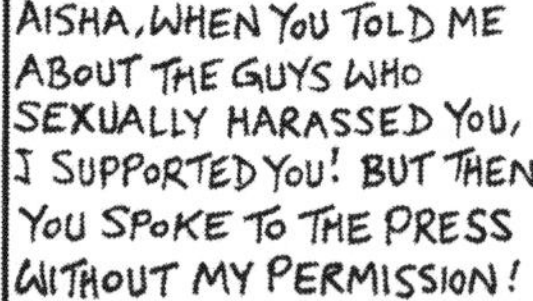

AISHA, WHEN YOU TOLD ME ABOUT THE GUYS WHO SEXUALLY HARASSED YOU, I SUPPORTED YOU! BUT THEN YOU SPOKE TO THE PRESS WITHOUT MY PERMISSION!

SO I'D HELP OTHER WOM--

YOU DISOBEYED ME!!
NO, NO! ANWAR, PLEASE DON'T!

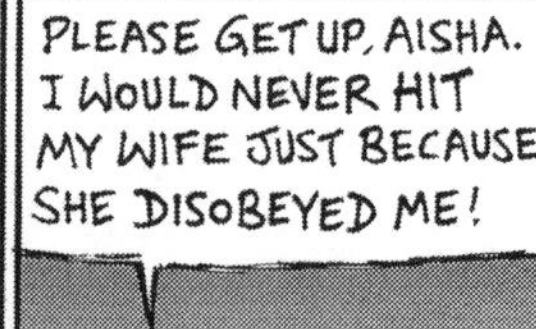

PLEASE GET UP, AISHA. I WOULD NEVER HIT MY WIFE JUST BECAUSE SHE DISOBEYED ME!

WOULD I?
WELL, SOME SCHOLARS SAY HIT, OTHERS SAY SPANK.

20 August 2009

ANWAR, MY REPORTERS APPROACHED YOUR WIFE WHEN THEY FOUND OUT SHE WAS SEXUALLY HARASSED ON THE STREET. SHE DIDN'T MEAN TO DISOBEY YOU WHEN SHE GAVE THAT INTERVIEW!

COME ON, ANWAR. I KNOW YOU STILL LOVE AISHA!
YES, OMAR. I DO. BUT A LITTLE LESS, AFTER WHAT SHE DID.

FORTUNATELY, MY LOVE FOR AISHA HAS DROPPED BY EXACTLY HALF...

...WHICH MEANS, IF NEED BE, I WILL TAKE ON A SECOND WIFE WITHOUT BEING UNFAIR TO HER.
WHAT?

26 August 2009

YOUR WIFE TELLS THE MEDIA ABOUT BEING HARASSED IN THE STREET, AND YOU WANT TO PUNISH HER BY MARRYING ANOTHER WOMAN?!
ANWAR, MY BROTHER LOOKS UP TO YOU. BUT NOW YOU'RE LETTING YOUR RAGE TAKE OVER! THAT'S NOT THE DEFINITION OF A GOOD MUSLIM!
OH, I SEE, OMAR! SO NOW YOU'RE GOD'S SPOKESMAN?
TELL ME, WHAT'S GOD SAYING TO ME RIGHT NOW?
HE SAYS, "THIS TIME THE INFIDEL'S GOT A POINT."

29 August 2009

BIG FALAFEL, WHY ARE EGYPTIANS SMILING ALL THE TIME?
THEY HAVE FAITH, NADA.
WELL, THEN THEY NEED A DOSE OF REALITY!
YOU'RE DOING WHAT YOU CAN AS A JOURNALIST.
IF I WERE DOING MY JOB RIGHT, THE PEOPLE WOULD KNOW WHERE THIS COUNTRY IS HEADED. THEN THEY'D WIPE THAT SMILE OFF THEIR FACES...
... AND START LAUGHING HYSTERICALLY!
FIN
النهاية
SERIES THREE STARTS 5 SEPTEMBER 2009
MY THANKS TO ALL READERS.

31 August 2009

AL KHAN III
5 SEPTEMBER 2009

PART THREE
Scary But Good

3 November 2009

CAN YOU BELIEVE THE AUDACITY OF THE RULING PARTY ?! ... PROMISING EGYPTIANS COMPETITIVE ELECTIONS AND SOCIAL JUSTICE!
THEY THINK THE PUBLIC IS STUPID! DON'T THEY FEAR AN ANGRY REVOLUTION?
WELL, AT LEAST THEY WERE TRUTHFUL ABOUT THE SOCIAL JUSTICE PART.
OMAR! SERIOUSLY?!
NADA, WHY WON'T YOU UNDERSTAND THAT CAPITALISM IS SOCIAL JUSTICE?
BECAUSE IT ONLY FAVORS THE POWERFUL!
AND A REVOLUTION WON'T?

5 September 2009

...AND THAT'S HOW ARCHAEOLOGISTS CAN RETROACTIVELY DETERMINE WHEN THE PYRAMIDS WERE BUILT!
WOW!! WHAT ELSE CAN ARCHAEOLOGISTS TELL US?
EVERYTHING! THEY CAN TELL US ALL ABOUT ANCIENT EGYPT!
CAN THEY TELL US HOW THE PHARAOHS RULED?
OF COURSE!
EVEN THE LAST PHARAOH?
DID I MENTION ARCHAEOLOGY IS ONLY A RETROACTIVE SCIENCE?
© 2009. Tarek Shahin. www.alkhancomics.com

7 September 2009

HOW CAN CONSTRUCTION WORK ON A METRO LINE CREATE SUCH A MASSIVE SINKHOLE?
CAIRO'S ROTTING INFRASTRUCTURE!
THE GOVERNMENT SAID IT WOULD FIX IT.
TOO LITTLE TOO LATE!
NADA, AT LEAST THEY'RE BUILDING A THIRD METRO LINE.
TOO LITTLE TOO LATE!
YUNAN, IT'S NOT ENOUGH TO ACCOMMODATE CAIRO'S POPULATION GROWTH!
...WHICH IS TOO MUCH TOO FAST!
© 2009. Tarek Shahin. www.alkhancomics.com

8 September 2009

OMAR, WHAT HAVE YOU DONE WITH MY MAGAZINE SINCE YOU TOOK OVER AS PUBLISHER?
I'VE REVOLUTIONIZED ALKHAN, GRANDFATHER! I'VE ADDED NEW DISTRIBUTION CHANNELS MORE BEFITTING THE TWENTY FIRST CENTURY!
YOU WOULDN'T UNDERSTAND.
WOW!
HOW COME I NEVER GET ANY ALKHAN "TWEETS?"
NO ONE USES BIRDS TO CARRY PAPER ANYMORE!
© 2009. Tarek Shahin. www.alkhancomics.com

9 September 2009

MARIAN, WE'RE BACK FROM OUR HONEYMOON! I THOUGHT WE'D INVITE THE MAGAZINE STAFF OVER FOR AN IFTAR.

YUNAN, WHAT IF THEY DON'T LIKE MY COOKING?
THEY'RE NOT MY MOTHER, THEY'RE OUR FRIENDS!

BESIDES, IF YOU WANT TO LEAD A HEALTHY LIFE, YOU MUST LEARN TO OVERCOME YOUR SHYNESS.
PERHAPS YOU'RE RIGHT.

SPEAKING OF OVERCOMING SHYNESS, YUNAN, WHEN EXACTLY DO YOU PLAN ON CONSUMMATING OUR MARRIAGE?!

10 September 2009

NADA, YOUR EDITORIAL ON THE ANNIVERSARY OF 9/11...
WHAT ABOUT IT, OMAR?

WORDS LIKE "TERROR" AND "INNOCENT LIVES." I KNOW YOU HATE IT WHEN I INTERFERE BUT YOUR WORDING IS TOO SOFT!

HOW ABOUT ADDING "DEVASTATING" TO "TERROR" AND "COUNTLESS" TO "INNOCENT LIVES?"

OH I DID! IN THE "HOW AMERICA REACTED" SECTION.

11 September 2009

GRANDFATHER, I KNOW THE MONTH OF RAMADAN CAN BE PARTICULARLY DIFFICULT FOR SOMEONE LIKE YOU.

HUH?! OMAR, ARE YOU SERIOUS?! YOU EXPECT ME TO BE FASTING? AT MY AGE?

I DIDN'T THINK SO. IN ANY CASE, I JUST WANTED YOU TO KNOW I'M HERE TO SUPPORT YOU.

ARE YOU FASTING, OMAR?
WHAT KIND OF SUPPORT WOULD THAT BE?

12 September 2009

THE JEWS DON'T WANT FAROUK HOSNI TO RUN THE UNESCO BECAUSE HE SAID HE'D BURN HEBREW BOOKS!!
NO GLOBAL UPROAR OVER HIS PAST COMMENTS AGAINST THE HEAD VEIL?
THAT WAS A PERSONAL STATEMENT. THIS WAS A POLITICAL ONE.
BESIDES, ANWAR, DON'T YOU THINK IT'S INSENSITIVE TO PUT "BURN" AND "HEBREW" IN THE SAME SENTENCE, GIVEN WHAT HAPPENED TO THE JEWISH PEOPLE?
HAPPENED?!! OMAR, IF YOU READ THE QURAN, YOU'D KNOW THAT JUDGEMENT DAY ISN'T UNTIL THE AFTERLIFE!

14 September 2009

A FEUD BETWEEN THE EGYPTIAN GOVERNMENT AND THE PRIVATE WASTE COLLECTION COMPANY HAS LEFT PILES OF GARBAGE ON THE STREETS OF CAIRO AND GIZA. HOW DO YOU FEEL?
IT'S ACTUALLY A GOOD THING. I USED TO BE ISOLATED BY THE PRIVATE SECTOR. NOW I'M HERE, AMONGST MY PEOPLE!!
BUT THE PEOPLE DON'T WANT YOU!
WHEN I GET BIG ENOUGH, THEY WILL LEARN TO RESPECT ME!!
RESPECT, YOU MEAN LOVE YOU OR FEAR YOU?
LADY, I'M A GIANT PILE OF GARBAGE! I CAN'T SMELL THE DIFFERENCE!

16 September 2009

SON, 'LAYLAT AL QADR' IS THE MOST SACRED OF NIGHTS! GOD GIVES US A WINDOW TO MAKE ALL OUR WISHES!!
MAY ALLAH FEED ALL THE MUSLIM POOR. MAY ALLAH BLESS ALL THE MUSLIM DEAD. MAY ALLAH HEAL ALL THE MUSLIM SICK.
BABA, WHY DON'T YOU WISH THE REST OF HUMANITY WELL?
BECAUSE THE WINDOW IS SMALL!
IS GOD?

17 September 2009

YOUR EXCELLENCY, YOU'RE TO MAKE A TELEVISION APPEARANCE ON THE FIRST DAY OF EID.
WHY?! IT'S A HOLIDAY!!

EGYPTIANS AT HOME WANT TO ASK THE MINISTER OF PROSPERITY QUESTIONS ON THE AIR!

LIKE WHAT?

THEY MAY ASK YOU ABOUT 2010.
IT'S TOO EARLY TO TELL.

THEY MAY ASK YOU ABOUT 2011.
IT'S TOO EARLY TO LIE.

25 September 2009

MAGED, IF YOU'RE BORED, READ A BOOK.
WHY, OMAR?

READING ENTERTAINS AND ELEVATES.
SO DOES SMOKING HASHISH!

I THOUGHT YOU QUIT THAT STUFF!
I DID! I'M JUST SAYING.

READ ABOUT HEALTH TO ALTER YOUR PERCEPTION!
READ ABOUT HASHISH!

28 September 2009

AL KHAN
JULY 2009
SPECIAL REPORT
"I WAS SEXUALLY HARASSED ON THE STREETS OF CAIRO"

ANWAR, ARE YOU STILL ANGRY?
AISHA, I TOLD YOU NOT TO SPEAK TO ANYONE ABOUT YOUR ORDEAL!

I TOLD YOU, I HAD TO! TO HELP OTHER WOMEN!
HELPING OTHER WOMEN IS MORE IMPORTANT THAN OBEYING YOUR HUSBAND?

I'M A WIFE SECOND AND A WOMAN FIRST!
YOU'RE A **MUSLIM** FIRST!!

29 September 2009

MY WIFE HAS DISOBEYED ME, YOUR EMINENCE!
THEN YOU OUGHT TO ABANDON HER IN BED.
BUT I CAN'T ABANDON MY NEEDS!
I CAN HOOK YOU UP.
WHAT?! I'M ALLOWED TO CHEAT ON MY WIFE?!
OF COURSE NOT!! MARRIAGE IS THE MOST SACRED OF UNIONS.
...?
YOU'RE ALLOWED FOUR SUCH THE MOST SACRED OF UNIONS.
© 2009. Tarek Shahin. www.alkhancomics.com

30 September 2009

I CAN'T AFFORD TO PAY FOR THIS VISIT, DR. ANWAR!
AGAIN?!! LISTEN, I HAVE SEVEN KIDS TO FEED!
PLEASE DR. ANWAR! I CAN'T FIND A JOB!
MAYBE IF YOU TRIED HARDER INSTEAD OF SITTING ON YOUR ASS!
LET THIS BE YOUR GIFT TO ME!
FINE! ... BUT GOD WOULD'VE REWARDED YOUR HARD WORK MORE THAN HE'LL REWARD MY CHARITY.
THEN LET THIS BE MY GIFT TO YOU!
© 2009. Tarek Shahin. www.alkhancomics.com

3 October 2009

YUNAN, YOU LOOK WEAK! YOUR WIFE IS NOT COOKING FOR YOU PROPERLY!!
MAMA, I'M FINE! MARIAN AND I ARE EXTREMELY HAPPY TOGETHER! MORE IMPORTANTLY....
WHO SAYS THE WIFE MUST COOK FOR HER HUSBAND?! MARIAN WANTS TO BE A PHOTOGRAPHER LIKE ME. I THINK A WOMAN SHOULD HAVE DREAMS AND HER HUSBAND SHOULD HELP AROUND THE HOME!!
DID YOUR FATHER TELL YOU TO THINK SUCH THINGS?!
SON, THERE IS NO CORRECT ANSWER TO THAT QUESTION!
© 2009. Tarek Shahin. www.alkhancomics.com

7 October 2009

AND TONIGHT EVERYONE IN THE AUDIENCE GETS A FREE CAAAAAAR!!
YAY! WOOHOO! WE LOVE YOU OPRAH!
CLAP! CLAP! CLAP!!! CLAP!! CLAP!!

MY FIRST GUEST IS A SOCIOLOGIST WHOSE BEST-SELLING BOOK ON WOMEN'S RIGHTS WAS BANNED IN HER HOME COUNTRY OF EGYPT AND ALSO EARNED HER A DEATH FATWA!

CLAP.

I SAID... IT EARNED HER A DEATH FAATWAAAAA!!
YAY! WOOHOO! WE LOVE YOU OPRAH!
CLAP! CLAP! CLAP!!! CLAP!! CLAP!!

8 October 2009

INDEED, OPRAH. AS A SOCIOLOGIST I'VE BEEN IN EXILE BECAUSE THE RESULTS OF MY STUDIES ARE AN INCONVENIENT TRUTH IN EGYPT AND THE ARAB WORLD!
DR. EBAA ANTAR
AUTHOR: "HAREM AND ME"

WOMEN THERE ARE NOT ALLOWED TO CHOOSE WHO TO LOVE, WHEN TO USE THE BATHROOM OR WHICH COLOR SHOES TO BUY!!

BUT DR. EBAA, HOW DID YOU CONDUCT YOUR RESEARCH WHEN YOU'VE BEEN AWAY FROM EGYPT FOR DECADES?
I DID WHAT ANY TRUE SCIENTIST WOULD!
Coming Up:
Kittens: How Many Is Too Cute?

YOU HYPOTHESIZED YOUR RESULTS?
NO! I BELIEVED IN THEM.

9 October 2009

WHAT IS IT, MEIN FUHRER?
REJOICE, ALIA! THE AZHAR SHEIKH IS ISSUING A CLEAR FATWA AGAINST THE VEIL!

HE'S BANNING THE FULL FACE VEIL - THE NIQAB, NOT THE HEAD VEIL WHICH I CHOOSE TO WEAR!

I'M NOT FOLLOWING.
YES, OMAR! SOME WOMEN CHOOSE NIQAB. I CHOOSE VEIL.

"CHOOSE VEIL" IS A CONTRADICTION IN TERMS.
SO IS "CLEAR FATWA."

15 October 2009

THE ENTIRE WORLD IS RAVING ABOUT DR. EBAA ANTAR'S SO-CALLED STUDY OF WOMEN'S ISSUES IN THE ARAB WORLD!
SHE WROTE IT SITTING ON HER SOFA IN THE STATES!

YOU DON'T CONDUCT A SOCIAL STUDY REMOTELY!!
I'M GOING TO REVIEW HER BOOK!
WHERE WILL YOU GET IT, NADA?
HER BOOK IS BANNED IN EGYPT!

THAT WAS QUICK, BIG FALAFEL. THANKS.
DID YOU FINISH READING HER NONSENSE?
HAREM AND ME
DR. EBAA ANTAR

I STOPPED READING AT THE CHAPTER ON HOW THE ARAB MAN TATTOOS THE NIQAB FULLY ON HIS SECOND WIFE AS SOON AS HIS FIRST WIFE GIVES BIRTH TO HER.

16 October 2009

YUNAN!
LONG TIME, MR. FARID!
I HAVE SOME NEWS.

OH, I KNOW! YOU LEFT YOUR JOB AT THE MAGAZINE?
I DIDN'T.

SO YOU NO LONGER FEAR MY GRANDSON IS ERASING THE CORE VALUES OF MY MAGAZINE?
I DO.

OH, I KNOW! YOU GOT MARRIED?
I DID.

17 October 2009

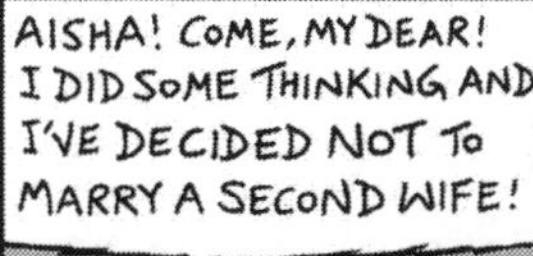
AISHA! COME, MY DEAR! I DID SOME THINKING AND I'VE DECIDED NOT TO MARRY A SECOND WIFE!

BECAUSE I REALIZED THAT EVEN IF YOU'VE SOMETIMES DISAPPOINTED ME,
I ONLY LOVE YOU!
WITH ALL OF MY HEART!
OH, ANWAR. AND I LOVE.... THAT YOU THINK YOU GET TO DECIDE IF AND WHEN TO CARE FOR MY FEELINGS.
WHICH IS WHY I AM DIVORCING YOU!

W-WWHAT?! H-H-HOW? HOW WILL YOU DO THAT?!
WITH ALL OF MY HEART.

23 October 2009

WAAAAAH! YA LAHWY! WHY? WHY IS MY WIFE LEAVING ME? NOOO!
ANWAR, DON'T DO THIS TO YOURSELF!
IT'S OVER, OMAR! IT'S OVER!
I CAN'T SEE YOU LIKE THIS! I'LL DO ANYTHING TO HELP!
ONLY GOD CAN HELP ME.
FINE. I'LL TRY TO PRAY FOR YOU! WHAT DO YOU USUALLY ASK GOD?
SAY SOMETHING, ANWAR! DON'T LEAVE ME ALONE WITH HIM!

27 October 2009

YUNAN, SON, IF YOU'RE HAVING TROUBLE PAYING FOR GROCERIES, WHY WON'T YOU LET ME HELP YOU?
NEVER! YOU AND MAMA SMOTHERED ME WELL INTO MY FORTIES. MY MARRIAGE IS THE ONLY THING I HAVE CONTROL OVER!
THAT MARRIAGE MAY NOT LAST IF YOU CAN'T PROVIDE FOR YOUR HOUSEHOLD!
MARIAN IS NOT LIKE THAT! SHE HAS A BIG HEART!
SO DID YOUR MOTHER. BUT THEN HER BELLY GOT JEALOUS!

28 October 2009

OMAR, I'M CARING FOR A HOUSEHOLD NOW AND I NEED A RAISE.
I WISH I COULD, YUNAN. BUT IF I GIVE YOU A RAISE I'LL BE ENDORSING THE SUBSIDY PROGRAM, WHICH THE EGYPTIAN GOVERNMENT IS CURRENTLY PHASING OUT.
NO...! AS A PRIVATE BUSINESS OWNER, GIVING ME A RAISE WOULD NEGATE MY NEED FOR A GOVERNMENT SUBSIDY!
I WISH I COULD, YUNAN. BUT IF I AGREE WITH YOUR ARGUMENT I'LL BE LISTENING TO LOGIC, WHICH THE EGYPTIAN GOVERNMENT IS CURRENTLY PHASING OUT.

30 October 2009

I'M REPORTING LIVE FROM CAIRO WHERE THE ANNUAL CONFERENCE OF EGYPT'S RULING NATIONAL DEMOCRATIC PARTY KICKS OFF TODAY.
CNN

ANALYSTS ARE DIVIDED AS TO WHETHER EGYPT'S PRESIDENT, WHO HAS RULED FOR 28 YEARS, WILL ANNOUNCE HIS CANDIDACY FOR YET ANOTHER TERM.
CNN

BUT EVEN MORE SIGNIFICANT IS THE DIVIDE AMONGST THE PEOPLE.
HERE ARE SOME VIEWS FROM THE VOTING PUBLIC:
CNN

SOME AMERICANS THINK ISRAEL IS SAFER WITH A MORE STABLE EGYPT, WHILE OTHER AMERICANS THINK CONGRESS SHOULD RECONSIDER AID.
BACK TO YOU...
CNN

5 November 2009*

HOW CAN WE ALLOW THE ONE THEY CALL BEYONCE TO SING IN EGYPT? THE GOVERNMENT WANTS TO CORRUPT OUR SOCIETY!

I'M PROUD TO SAY I'VE NEVER HEARD HER SONGS. BUT IF IT'S TRUE THAT SHE DANCES THEN SHE IS PURE EVIL!

WE SHOULD TEACH OUR SONS LOVE, NOT LUST!
MY OWN SON THOUGHT HE LOVED A GIRL AT SCHOOL!

I TOLD HIM IF YOU LIKED IT THEN YOU SHOULD'VE PUT A RING ON IT!!!

7 November 2009

HEY! YOU! Ms. NADA! YOU RUINED MY MARRIAGE!
EXCUSE ME? DO I KNOW YOU?
YOU INTERVIEWED ME FOR YOUR STORY ON VICTIMS OF SEXUAL HARASSMENT ON THE STREETS OF CAIRO.

OH!! AISHA! I COULDN'T RECOGNIZE YOU BECAUSE OF THE...
I SUPPOSE WE ALL LOOK ALIKE TO YOU!

NO, NO. I DIDN'T MEAN TO SAY IT LIKE THAT!
RELAX! TECHNICALLY IT'S A COMPLIMENT.

Notes by the author:

* "Put A Ring On It" was a 2009 hit by US singer Beyonce.

9 November 2009

WHEN I INTERVIEWED AISHA I MEANT TO SHED LIGHT ON WOMEN'S ISSUES, NOT DIVIDE HER FAMILY!
AM I CROSSING THE LINE AS A JOURNALIST?
NADA, YOU HATED DR. EBAA'S BOOK ON WOMEN BECAUSE IT WAS POORLY RESEARCHED.
YOUR DILIGENCE STANDS OUT BUT IT'S NOT WITHOUT ITS CONSEQUENCES!
BIG FALAFEL, WHY DOES THE TRUTH COME AT SUCH A HIGH PRICE?!
BECAUSE IT'S HARD TO FIND!
SUPPLY IS FALLING.
THEN I MUST FIGHT TO UNRAVEL MORE TRUTHS!
NOT REALLY. DEMAND IS FALLING FASTER.
© 2009. Tarek Shahin. www.alkhancomics.com

10 November 2009

...WHICH IS SCIENTIFIC PROOF THAT AMERICA'S DINOSAURS WERE ROMAN CATHOLIC!
YOU'RE WATCHING FOX NEWS.
OUR NEXT GUEST IS ACCLAIMED EGYPTIAN-BORN AUTHOR DR. EBAA ANTAR...
DR. EBAA, YOUR BOOK ON ARAB WOMEN IS BANNED IN THE ARAB WORLD. REVIEWS HAVE BEEN POSITIVE HERE IN THE WEST.
DO YOU PLAN TO RETURN TO EGYPT?
NEVER!! THERE'S A DEATH FATWA ON MY HEAD!
WELL, THE BOOK IS AWESOME! PLEASE DON'T PAY ATTENTION TO THAT ONE BAD REVIEW.
WAIT! WHAT BAD REVIEW? WHERE?
SOME LOCAL MAGAZINE IN CAIRO. IT WAS WRITTEN BY THE EDITOR, NADA SOMETHING.
ARE YOU NADA SOMETHING?
© 2009. Tarek Shahin. www.alkhancomics.com

11 November 2009

WOW, NADA! EGYPT HAS REALLY CHANGED SINCE I LEFT!
THAT'S WHY I ATTACKED YOUR BOOK, DR. EBAA! YOU CAN'T JUST MAKE ASSUMPTIONS ABOUT WOMEN'S ISSUES HERE WITHOUT EVEN VISITING!
WHAT'S THAT OVER THERE? IS THAT NEW?
CAIRO TOWER? IT WAS BUILT IN THE FIFTIES!
WOW! HOW LONG HAVE YOU BEEN GONE?!
AND WHAT'S THAT OVER THERE? IS THAT NEW?
THE SPHINX?
© 2009. Tarek Shahin. www.alkhancomics.com

12 November 2009

SALAM ALAIKOM, ANWAR.
OH MY GOD! AISHA! YOU'RE BACK!

LISTEN CAREFULLY, ANWAR! I'M GOING TO STAY AND MAKE THIS MARRIAGE WORK!
BUT ONLY BECAUSE I DON'T WANT MY CHILDREN TO GROW UP IN A TORN FAMILY!

ONLY FOR THE KIDS? FINE! BUT PLEASE TELL ME THERE'S NO HATRED!
I'M STANDING IN OUR HOME!
ISN'T THAT WHAT YOU WANTED?

NO, I WANT YOU SLEEPING IN MY BED!
FINE! BUT PLEASE TELL ME THERE'S NO NUDITY.

13 November 2009

GOD, PLEASE LET EGYPT WIN AGAINST ALGERIA TOMORROW TO QUALIFY FOR THE FIFA WORLD CUP!

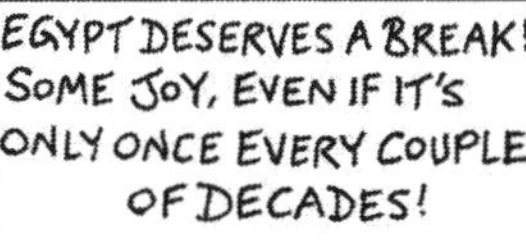
EGYPT DESERVES A BREAK! SOME JOY, EVEN IF IT'S ONLY ONCE EVERY COUPLE OF DECADES!

IF WE DON'T QUALIFY WE'LL LOSE HOPE IN OURSELVES.
IN OUR GOVERNMENT.
IN OUR PRESENT.
IN OUR FUTURE.
AND ALL THAT'LL BE LEFT IS PRAYER.
SO PLEASE, GOD....

14 November 2009

YOUR EXCELLENCY, WE NEED YOU TO PRE-TAPE THE CABINET'S MESSAGE TO EGYPT'S FOOTBALL TEAM, CONGRATULATING THEM ON THEIR WORLD CUP QUALIFYING MATCH.

YOU PLAYED WELL! AND EVERY STEP OF THE WAY THE HEART OF THE PRESIDENT WAS WITH YOU.

NOW WE NEED TO TAPE AN ALTERNATE VERSION IN CASE THE TEAM LOSES THE MATCH.

YOU PLAYED WELL! AND EVERY STEP OF THE WAY THE HEARTS OF THE CABINET OF MINISTERS WERE WITH YOU.

17 November 2009

AISHA, EVER SINCE WE'VE RECONCILED YOU HAVE NOT RESUMED YOUR ROLE AS A WIFE!

A MAN HAS A BASIC NEED! IF YOU WON'T DO IT FOR ME I'LL HAVE TO DO IT TO MYSELF!
BECAUSE I CAN'T CONTROL MY BODY!

SO COULD YOU PLEASE TEACH ME HOW TO CUT MY TOENAILS?

18 November 2009

SEE, UNLIKE YOU, DR. EBAA, I'VE ACTUALLY LIVED HERE! SO MY REPORTS ON ARAB WOMEN AND SOCIETY HAVE CREDIBILITY!

NADA, TODAY WE LIVE IN A VIRTUAL WORLD, WHERE INFORMATION TECHNOLOGY HAS OPENED THE BORDERS CLOSED BY TERRORISM.

I'VE DONE LOTS OF STUDIES ON WORLD CULTURES FROM MY BASE IN THE STATES.
ONE OF THEM WAS SO GOOD IT WAS A BIG HIT IN THE WHITE HOUSE!

LET ME GUESS: "THE IRAQIS WILL GREET US AS LIBERATORS."
YOU'RE SAYING IT WAS A HIT HERE TOO?

20 November 2009

AND ALGERIA BEATS EGYPT TO QUALIFY FOR THE FIFA WORLD CUP!!!

WHY WOULD A GAME LEAD TO SUCH BARBARIC VIOLENCE AMONGST FANS?
BECAUSE WE ARE ARABS.

I GUESS YOU'RE ANGRY THAT EGYPT DIDN'T QUALIFY.
OF COURSE!

SO HOW COME YOU SAID IF EGYPT LOST YOU WOULD SUPPORT ALGERIA IN THE WORLD CUP?
BECAUSE WE ARE ARABS.

21 November 2009

NADA, I'VE DECIDED TO DO FIELD RESEARCH IN CAIRO. I CAN NO LONGER STUDY THIS COMPLEX SOCIETY FROM A FAR!
GLAD TO HEAR IT, DR. EBAA.
BUT I'M NOT SAFE HERE! REMEMBER - THERE WAS A DEATH FATWA ISSUED AGAINST ME BY ISLAMIST CLERICS BECAUSE OF MY WRITINGS!
STOP BEING SELF-IMPORTANT, DR. EBAA! YOU'RE NOT THE ONLY ONE. CRAZY FATWAS ARE ISSUED EVERY DAY!
SO HOW DO YOU TELL IF A FATWA IS SERIOUS?
BY THE SIZE OF OF THE ISSUING CAVE.
© 2009. Tarek Shahin. www.alkhancomics.com

23 November 2009

AISHA CAME BACK BUT SHE DOESN'T TREAT ME AS A HUSBAND ANYMORE!
THE TRUTH IS, OMAR, I'VE ALREADY PROPOSED TO A WOMAN, WHO HAS AGREED TO BE MY SECOND WIFE.
ANWAR! AGAIN? THAT WAS THE REASON AISHA LEFT YOU IN THE FIRST PLACE!
NO! SHE FEARED I'D BRING A STRANGER INTO OUR HOME! SHE FELT BETRAYED!
THAT'S WHY I PROPOSED TO HER BEST FRIEND. SO SHE WOULDN'T FEEL BETRAYED!
© 2009. Tarek Shahin. www.alkhancomics.com

24 November 2009

SO AS I SAID, AISHA, I LOVE YOU AND I WANT YOU TO APPROVE MY SECOND MARRIAGE.
ANWAR, I LEFT YOU!! AND THEN I CAME BACK TO SAVE OUR FAMILY! AND THIS IS HOW YOU REPAY ME?!!
THIS WILL WORK, AISHA. YOU AND I ARE BEST FRIENDS!
YOU SHUT UP! I TRUSTED YOU!
ANWAR, YOU TOLD ME ONLY YOU CAN YELL IN OUR HOME!
NO! I SAID FIRST WIVES AND OLDER!
© 2009. Tarek Shahin. www.alkhancomics.com

30 November 2009

I'M NO EXPERT BUT I'M SURPRISED DUBAI HAS DEBT PROBLEMS!
DUBAI HAS NO OIL. THEY RELIED ON PRE-CRISIS LIQUIDITY.
DUBAI CRISIS
OMAR, DIDN'T YOU ONCE SAY YOU HELPED LEND MONEY TO DUBAI BACK WHEN YOU WERE A BANKER IN LONDON?
MAYBE YOU'RE TO BLAME! YOU SHOULD HAVE ASKED MORE QUESTIONS!
YUNAN, WE DID ASK QUESTIONS!
LONDON: 2005
WHY DO WE WANT TO BUILD THE WORLD'S TALLEST STEEL STRUCTURE?
YES! WHY USE STEEL WHEN YOU CAN USE DIAMOND?

1 December 2009

MAY GOD BLESS THIS MARRIAGE AND MAY YOU TREAT BOTH WIVES EQUALLY.
DR. ANWAR, ARE YOUR WITNESSES READY?
MATE, I DON'T THINK I'M ELIGIBLE!
WHY NOT, BROTHER LEVY? I WANT MY MUSLIM WITNESS TO BE ONE OF US.
ANWAR, I'VE BEEN WANTING TO CONFESS SOMETHING TO YOU FOR SOME TIME.
MY NAME IS NOAH COHEN LEVY KING, AND I'M....
YOUR EMINENCE, CAN WE STILL PROCEED IF MY WITNESS IS NEUTRAL ON THE EGYPT-ALGERIA FOOTBALL FEUD?

2 December 2009

YOU WERE BEAUTIFUL AT THE WEDDING CEREMONY.
I'M GLAD WE'RE NOW ALONE SO I CAN FINALLY SEE YOUR FACE.
WAIT... WHAT'S THAT UNDERNEATH YOUR DRESS?
WHAT ARE THESE PAPER NOTES?!
"THE SUBJECT APPROACHES ME WITH THE LUST OF A NEWLYWED. BUT THE SUBJECT IS RESTRAINED. PERHAPS FEELINGS OF GUILT TOWARDS HIS FIRST WIFE..."
WHAT IS THIS?! WHO ARE YOU WRITING THIS FOR?
OH SHIT! I MEAN... UH... DOES THE SUBJECT NOT LIKE MY... UH... POETRY?

3 December 2009

TEN DAYS EARLIER...
THIS IS AISHA. AISHA, THIS IS DR. EBAA ANTAR. I TOLD HER THAT YOU AND YOUR HUSBAND ANWAR ARE PERFECT FOR HER RESEARCH ON THE PLIGHT OF EGYPTIAN WOMEN.
NO! NO! MS. NADA, THE LAST TIME I OPENED MY DOORS IT DIVIDED MY FAMILY!
AISHA, SHE JUST WANTS TO CHAT TO YOU! WHAT'S THE WORST THAT CAN HAPPEN?

THESE PAPERS I FOUND LOOK LIKE RESEARCH NOTES!
NO, IT'S...UH.. ...POETRY! I WROTE IT FOR OUR WEDDING NIGHT, ANWAR!

WELL, IT'S BEAUTIFUL. JUST LIKE YOU, EBAA!

4 December 2009

PREVIOUSLY ON 'AL KHAN'...
AISHA CAME BACK BUT SHE DOESN'T TREAT ME AS A HUSBAND ANYMORE!
I PROPOSED TO HER FRIEND TO BE MY SECOND WIFE.

DR. EBAA, EVEN IF I SAY YES, ANWAR WON'T AGREE TO BEING PART OF YOUR SOCIAL RESEARCH! HE WON'T EVEN LOOK AT A WOMAN IF HER FACE ISN'T COVERED!

SALAM ALAIKOM, AISHA. WHO'S THIS?
ANWAR, THIS IS DR. EBAA, MY FRIEND FROM THE MOSQUE.
SHE'S ONLY VISITING.

DOCTOR? SO AM I. IS AISHA NOT FEELING WELL?
SHE HAS 'SELFISHLY WANT THIS MAN ALL TO MYSELF' SYNDROME.
WHAT?!! HEY!! I TRUSTED YOU!!

5 December 2009

HELLO SIR. MAY I ASK WHY YOU VOTED AGAINST THE BUILDING OF MINARETS HERE IN SWITZERLAND?

IT WAS WRONG BUT I HAD TO. I LOVE MY MUSLIM FRIENDS.
BUT I WANT TO DISCOURAGE THE MUSLIMS WHO FLOCK TO EUROPE THESE DAYS ONLY TO SPREAD SHARIA LAW!

I THINK SHARIA LAW WILL DESTROY THE FREEDOMS MY FAMILY AND I ENJOY.
IF YOU WANT SHARIA, STAY IN A MUSLIM COUNTRY.

THANK YOU, SIR. MAY I HAVE YOUR NAME?
AHMED. I HOPE ALLAH FORGIVES ME.

7 December 2009

SALAM ALAIKOM. ARE YOU SHIITE?
WHAT?! NO! SUNNI OF COURSE!

SO YOU WOULDN'T WANT IRAN'S RULER TO TAKE OVER EGYPT?
NO. I GUESS THAT WOULD BE DANGEROUS.

YOU'RE SAYING IT WOULD BE DANGEROUS TO HAVE A PRESIDENT WHO'S AN EXPERT ON ATOMIC ENERGY.

EGYPTIAN STATE MEDIA SURVEYS HAVE FOUND OVERWHELMING OBJECTION TO FORMER IAEA DIRECTOR DR. MOHAMED ELBARADEI'S SUPPOSED BID FOR PRESIDENT.

8 December 2009

DR. EBAA, WHEN I SUGGESTED YOU STUDY AISHA I DID NOT MEAN MARRY HER HUSBAND!!!

ANWAR DOESN'T KNOW MY BOOKS. MARRYING HIM IS THE PERFECT WAY FOR ME TO STUDY POLYGAMY WHILST HIDING FROM THE ISLAMISTS WHO WANT TO KILL ME!

AS IF POOR AISHA HASN'T SUFFERED ENOUGH IN THIS MARRIAGE!
SEE, NADA, AS A SECOND WIFE I CAN CARRY SOME OF THE LOAD!

YOU DON'T UNDERSTAND. I'M TALKING PAIN!
OH, IT'S COOL. I'LL JUST TELL ANWAR I'M NOT INTO THAT KIND OF THING.

11 December 2009

SO DR. EBAA MARRIED MY HUSBAND BECAUSE YOU TOLD HER HER BOOKS LACKED PROPER FIELD RESEARCH?

AISHA, I DIDN'T MEAN FOR ANY OF THIS TO HAPPEN!
I ACCEPT GOD'S WILL.
BUT STILL...

MS. NADA, JUST BECAUSE I'M A POOR, SIMPLE WOMAN DOESN'T GIVE YOU JOURNALISTS AND SOCIAL SCIENTISTS THE RIGHT TO PUT MY FAMILY UNDER YOUR MICROSCOPE!

CAN YOU FIND A SMALL PLACE IN YOUR HEART THAT FORGIVES ME?
CAN I BORROW YOUR MICROSCOPE?

16 December 2009

THE EGYPTIAN MOVEMENT FOR CHANGE ('KEFAYA') ARE BOYCOTTING THE ELECTIONS?
THEY WON'T SUPPORT ELECTIONS THAT ARE CONSTITUTIONALLY FLAWED AND UNFAIR.

I UNDERSTAND, NADA. BUT THEY'LL ELECT AN 'ALTERNATIVE' PRESIDENT? CHOSEN BY WHOM?
CHOSEN BY THE PEOPLE.

YOU MEAN CHOSEN BY THE SOCIALIST LEADERS OF 'KEFAYA?'
OMAR, IT WAS THE CAPITALIST BUSINESS LEADERS WHO BACKED THE UNJUST RULING REGIME!!

AS AN ALTERNATIVE!

19 December 2009

YUNAN, YOU LOOK HEALTHY AND HAPPY! IT SEEMS MARIAN IS TAKING GOOD CARE OF YOU. SHE'S A DECENT PERSON.

MAMA, STOP BEING A STEREOTYPE OF EGYPTIAN MOTHERS-IN-LAW!!

HOW AM I A BAD MOTHER-IN-LAW?! I'M STARTING TO SAY NICE THINGS ABOUT YOUR WIFE!
I DON'T WANT YOU TO SAY NICE THINGS ABOUT HER!

I WANT YOU TO SAY NICE THINGS TO HER!!

22 December 2009

BABA, THIS DECADE HAD ITS UPS AND DOWNS. THE DECADE WAS GOOD TO ME AT THE HEIGHT OF MY LONDON CAREER, WHEN I THOUGHT JANE WAS THE ONE.

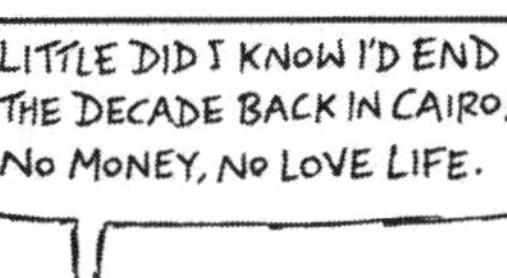

LITTLE DID I KNOW I'D END THE DECADE BACK IN CAIRO, NO MONEY, NO LOVE LIFE.

ON THE OTHER HAND, MAGED, MAMA AND GRANDFATHER SAY THEIR DECADE GOT BETTER WHEN I CAME BACK INTO THEIR LIVES.

DO YOU THINK IN THE NEXT DECADE SOMEONE LIKE ME CAN COME INTO MY LIFE?

23 December 2009

OK, I'LL BE THE EARLY 2000s.
AND I'LL BE THE LATE 2000s.
TERROR. WAR?
PEACE. PRIZE?
ISLAM. CHINA?
CHINA. GOD?
FREEDOM. PRIVACY?
CHANGE. MY PRIVACY SETTINGS?
SPECIAL GUEST WRITER: OMAIMA AL SEESI

24 December 2009

MOTHER, YOU'RE DOING A BELLY DANCING NEW YEAR'S SHOW ON THE NILE?
AT YOUR AGE?!
NAHED HABIB NEW YEAR
2010
NADA, ORIENTAL DANCING IS A FULL-ROUNDED ART. WHAT I LACK IN YOUTH I MAKE UP FOR IN CURVES!
YOU'RE JUST JEALOUS BECAUSE YOU'RE A JOURNALIST AND YOU'LL NEVER HAVE THE LOVE I GET AS AN ARTIST.
WHAT I LACK IN LOUD, DRUNK TOURISTS I MAKE UP FOR IN QUIET, ANGRY LOCAL READERS.

26 December 2009

THANKS FOR TAKING ME OUT, OMAR.
CAIRO CHANGES EVERY TIME I SEE IT.
SHE'S A BEAUTY.
BUT THE RICH ARE RICHER. AND THE POOR ARE POORER.
MAY I COME VISIT THE MAGAZINE I FOUNDED DECADES AGO?
MORE THAN WELCOME, GRANDFATHER!
WILL I FIND THAT YOU'VE MADE THE EDITORS AND REPORTERS HAPPY?
I ASSURE YOU. THE POOR ARE NOT ANY POORER.

28 December 2009

MR. FARID IS COMING TO VISIT AL KHAN? THIS AFTERNOON?
NADA, YOU'LL TELL MY GRANDFATHER THAT AS PUBLISHER I NEVER INTERFERE IN THE EDITORIAL CONTENT.

OMAR, LAST WEEK YOU CHANGED MY STORY HEADLINE!!
I DIDN'T CHANGE A SINGLE WORD!

Egyptian masses demanding reason for high food prices
YES, BUT YOU ADDED A COMMA!

Egyptian masses demanding, reason for high food prices
IT'S JUST A COMMA!

© 2009. Tarek Shahin. www.alkhancomics.com

29 December 2009

AISHA, HOW DO I KNOW IF ANWAR IS TICKLISH WITHOUT UPSETTING HIM IN THE PROCESS?
EBAA, LEAVE ME ALONE!

I WANT TO BE A GOOD SECOND WIFE! PLEASE HELP ME!
YOU CAN JUST ASK ME WHAT UPSETS ANWAR!

I'M A SCIENTIST! I'M LESS INTERESTED IN THE 'WHAT.' I'M MUCH MORE INTERESTED IN THE 'HOW.'
FINE! SO TICKLE HIM AND FIND OUT IN THE PROCESS!

WHAT IF HE KICKS ME?
I'M MUCH MORE INTERESTED IN THE 'HOW HARD.'

© 2009. Tarek Shahin. www.alkhancomics.com

30 December 2009

STAFF MEMBERS OF ALKHAN, PLEASE WELCOME BACK THE FOUNDER OF OUR GREAT MAGAZINE, MR. FARID, MY GRANDFATHER!!
GUYS WHY ARE SO MANY PHONES RINGING?
RING! RING!

ALO! HELLO, MARIAN! YUNAN WILL CALL YOU BACK. WE'RE WAITING FOR MY... WHAT?!
ALO! HELLO, MAGED! YOUR BROTHER IS ON THE PHONE. WHAT?!

YUNAN! YOUR WIFE'S PREGNANT!
OMAR, YOUR GRANDFATHER DIED.

ALO! OMAR, ARE YOU STILL THERE? MY CONDOLENCES.
ALO! YUNAN, ARE YOU STILL THERE? CONGRATULATIONS.

© 2009. Tarek Shahin. www.alkhancomics.com

31 December 2009

GOODBYE LAST YEAR

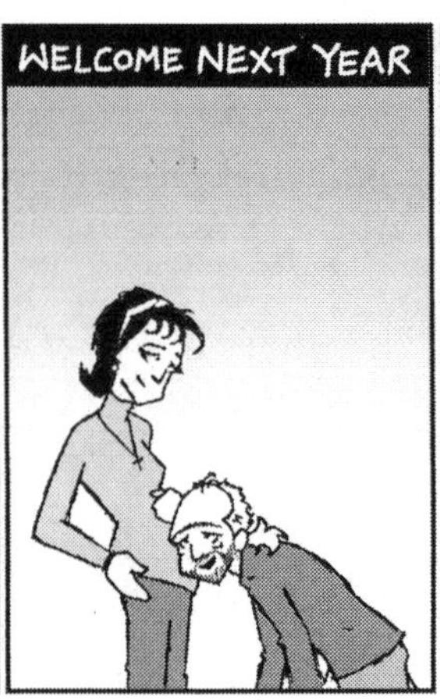
WELCOME NEXT YEAR

MAY IT BRING JOY
عام
سعيد
2010
HAPPY NEW YEAR 2010

TO ALL.

2 January 2010

2010 IS THE FIRST OF TWO POTENTIALLY GAME-CHANGING ELECTION YEARS IN EGYPT.
YOUNG LADY, DID YOU APPLY FOR A VOTING CARD?

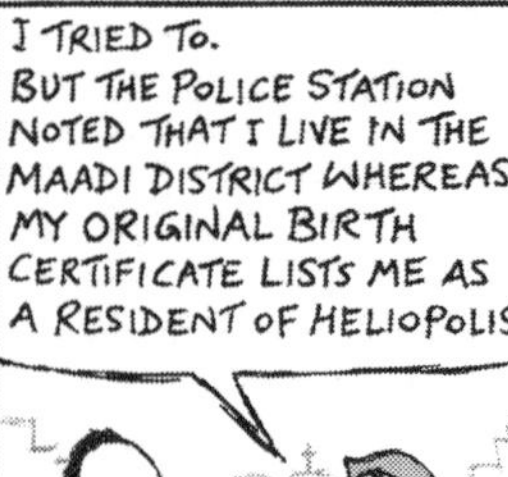
I TRIED TO.
BUT THE POLICE STATION NOTED THAT I LIVE IN THE MAADI DISTRICT WHEREAS MY ORIGINAL BIRTH CERTIFICATE LISTS ME AS A RESIDENT OF HELIOPOLIS.

YOU THINK THE GOVERNMENT IS USING BUREAUCRACY TO DEFLECT POTENTIAL OPPOSITION VOTERS?

I DON'T KNOW.
THEY ALSO NOTED THAT I'M A PhD STUDENT WHEREAS MY ORIGINAL BIRTH CERTIFICATE LISTS ME AS A NEWBORN.

4 January 2010

OMAR, I KNOW YOU LOVED YOUR GRANDFATHER.
GOD WILLING, HE WILL BE IN HEAVEN.
THANKS, ANWAR.

HE WAS A GOOD MAN. HE'LL BE IN OUR MEMORIES.
NO. NOT MEMORIES.
HEAVEN!

MAYBE SOME OF US DON'T BELIEVE IN A HEAVEN!!
HEAVEN IS A DECISION FOR GOD, NOT US.

YOU'RE SAYING I CAN GO TO HEAVEN TOO?
OF COURSE!
YOU'RE A FRIEND!

8 January 2010

YOUR EXCELLENCY, HAMAS CONTINUE TO ATTACK EGYPT'S BORDER WITH GAZA!
WE'LL ISSUE A HARSH WARNING!

WAR WITH HAMAS?! THE WHOLE POINT OF SUFFOCATING THE GAZANS WAS TO SPEED UP THE PEACE PROCESS!

WE COULD ALWAYS JUST ALLOW MORE AID TO GO THROUGH.
BUT THAT WOULD STRENGTHEN HAMAS' GRIP ON GAZA!

WE COULD ALWAYS MOVE MORE TROOPS TO THE BORDER.
BUT THAT WOULD WEAKEN OUR GRIP ON EGYPT!

9 January 2010

SIX COPTIC CHRISTIANS KILLED BY MUSLIMS? SHAMEFUL! ISLAM CONDEMNS THIS!
I DO HOPE SO, ANWAR!
DRIVE BY SHOOTING SIX COPTS

OMAR, STOP BLAMING RELIGION! I BLAME OUR SECULAR GOVERNMENT FOR THE SECTARIANISM!

CHRISTIANS IN EGYPT DESERVE TO FEEL SAFE. THAT IS THEIR RIGHT AS EQUAL CITIZENS!

HOW IS THE GOVERNMENT GOING TO FUND ALL OF THIS EQUALITY WHEN CHRISTIANS AND MUSLIMS ARE STILL PAYING EQUAL RATES OF TAX?!

12 January 2010

MARIAN!!! COME HERE, GIVE ME A HUG, MY PRECIOUS ANGEL!

I SEE, MAMA. LAST WEEK SHE WAS THAT WOMAN WHO MARRIED YOUR SON. AND NOW THAT SHE'S PREGNANT WITH YOUR GRANDCHILD, SHE'S YOUR PRECIOUS ANGEL?

YUNAN, DON'T SAY THAT! THERE ARE MORE REASONS TO LOVE MY DAUGHTER-IN-LAW THAN JUST A GRANDCHILD!!

SO HURRY UP AND GET HER PREGNANT WITH THE SECOND AND THIRD REASONS!

13 January 2010

OMAR, YOUR GRANDFATHER AND I HAD OUR DISAGREEMENTS. BUT WE'RE A FAMILY.
THANKS FOR DRIVING ALL THE WAY FROM THE VILLAGE, UNCLE AMIN.

BEFORE I LEAVE, ARE YOU ABSOLUTELY SURE YOU DON'T NEED ANYTHING?
I'D BE INTERESTED TO KNOW WHAT THE DISPUTE WAS ABOUT.

I WOULDN'T CALL IT A DISPUTE! YOUR GRANDFATHER AND I HAD A TINY DIFFERENCE IN OPINION! YOU THINK I EVEN REMEMBER WHAT IT WAS ABOUT?!

ANYWAY, BEFORE I LEAVE, ARE YOU ABSOLUTELY SURE HE'S DEAD?

14 January 2010

AISHA, IT'S MY DUTY TO BALANCE BETWEEN WIVES. SO I'LL SPEND SOME NIGHTS WITH EBAA AND SOME NIGHTS WITH YOU.

PLEASE, ANWAR! SPEND ALL YOUR TIME WITH HER. JUST STAY AWAY FROM ME!
BUT YOU HAVE NEEDS!

YOU THINK YOU KNOW ANYTHING ABOUT MY NEEDS?!
I DO, AISHA! AFTER OUR MANY YEARS OF MARRIAGE, YOU THINK I HAVE LEARNED NOTHING?!

A WOMAN NEEDS HER MAN AS MUCH AS A MAN NEEDS HIS WOMEN.

15 January 2010

YOUR UNCLE HAD A FALLING OUT WITH MY FATHER A FEW YEARS AGO. THE ONLY REASON HE STILL SPEAKS TO ME IS BECAUSE I'M HIS BROTHER'S WIDOW.

MAMA, THAT'S WHY I WANT TO VISIT HIM IN THE VILLAGE. BABA ALWAYS SAID 'FAMILY FIRST.' AND I HAVEN'T SEEN OUR RELATIVES SINCE I CAME BACK FROM LONDON!

WELL, OMAR, IF YOU'RE TRYING TO BOND WITH YOUR ROOTS, PERHAPS YOU SHOULD SCALE DOWN THIS 'LONDON LOOK!'
IT'S JUST A REGULAR COAT! I MUST PROTECT MY BODY FROM THE COLD!

AND MY HEAD FROM THE MOSQUITOES!

16 January 2010

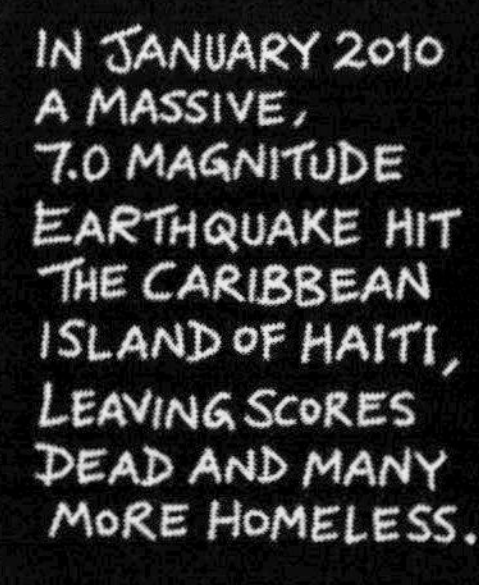

IN JANUARY 2010 A MASSIVE, 7.0 MAGNITUDE EARTHQUAKE HIT THE CARIBBEAN ISLAND OF HAITI, LEAVING SCORES DEAD AND MANY MORE HOMELESS.

THE NUMBER OF CASUALTIES AND THE EXTENT OF THE DEVASTATION RIVAL THE ASIAN TSUNAMI OF 2004 AND HURRICANE KATRINA IN THE STATES IN 2005.

EGYPT HAS NOT HAD A NATURAL DISASTER IN ALMOST 20 YEARS.

LUCK?

VOTE FOR THE NATIONAL DEMOCRATIC PARTY.
STABILITY.

19 January 2010

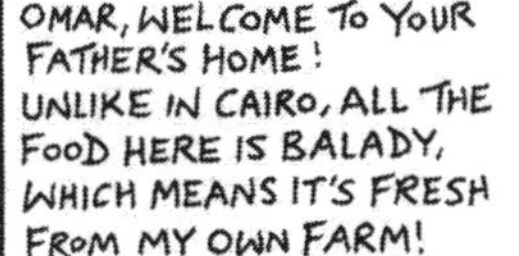

OMAR, WELCOME TO YOUR FATHER'S HOME! UNLIKE IN CAIRO, ALL THE FOOD HERE IS BALADY, WHICH MEANS IT'S FRESH FROM MY OWN FARM!

SOUNDS YUM!

I'LL HAVE THEM COOK THE RICE. MEANWHILE, YOU SLAUGHTER THE CHICKEN.
DO WHAT?!

I... UH... I'VE NEVER DONE THIS BEFORE.
IT'S MY FIRST TIME TOO. OBVIOUSLY.

I UNDERSTAND THERE'S A HALAL WAY TO DO THIS.
OH, SO YOU JUST ASSUME A CHICK IS MUSLIM IF SHE'S STILL INTACT?

20 January 2010

SEE, OMAR, I DIVIDED MY VAST FARMLAND INTO SMALL PARCELS.
THAT WAY I'M NOT LIMITED BY THE GOVERNMENT'S SUBSIDY QUOTA!

YOU MEAN THE GOVERNMENT IS PAYING FOR YOUR FERTILIZER?
WE CALL IT PAYING BACK! FOR OUR COOPERATION DURING NASSER'S SOCIALST REFORMS.

BUT, STILL, UNCLE AMIN, YOU'RE STEALING FROM THE GOVERNMENT!
I'M NOT TAKING MORE FERTILIZER. JUST MORE SUBSIDIES.

WHAT'S THE DIFFERENCE?! IT'S STILL STEALING FROM THE GOVERNMENT!
NO! ONLY FROM THE PEOPLE! WE CALL THAT STEALING BACK.

22 January 2010

WITH ONLINE CITIZEN MEDIA, PHOTOJOURNALISM WILL NO LONGER BE A PAYING JOB! IN A FEW YEARS, MY SKILLS WILL BE FREE!
STOP WORRYING ABOUT OUR BABY. IT'S STILL EARLY!
TOYS! SCHOOL! NONE OF IT'S FREE!
YUNAN, WHEN YOU TALK ABOUT MONEY LIKE THIS, YOU LOSE YOUR CHARM.
FINE, MARIAN. I'LL STOP.
YES!! YOUR CHARM! IT'S BACK!!
IT'S FREE.
© 2010. Tarek Shahin. www.alkhancomics.com

23 January 2010

OMAR, I'M RUNNING AGAIN FOR PARLIAMENT LATER THIS YEAR.
UNCLE AMIN, WHY DID YOU LOSE IN 2005?
YOUR GRANDFATHER REFUSED TO APOLOGIZE FOR AN ARTICLE IN ALKHAN MAGAZINE WHICH HAD OFFENDED THE VILLAGERS HERE!
HE SAID 'EDITORIAL FREEDOM' WAS MORE SACRED THAN OUR FAMILY TIES!
SO THE VILLAGERS WOULD HAVE VOTED FOR YOU IF ONLY HE'D APOLOGIZED?
LUCKILY THIS YEAR HE'S DEAD.
AND YOU'RE THE NEW PUBLISHER!
SO YOU CAN EITHER HELP YOUR UNCLE WIN THIS YEAR, OR YOU CAN DEFY GOD'S WILL, LIKE YOUR GRANDFATHER DID, AND HELP THE MUSLIM BROTHERHOOD WIN AGAIN!
© 2010. Tarek Shahin. www.alkhancomics.com

25 January 2010*

YOUR EXCELLENCY, THE MINISTRY OF PROSPERITY IS ACCUSED OF DOWNPLAYING THE DEADLY FLOOD IN SINAI AND ASWAN.
MAYBE WE SHOULD REVISE OUR OFFICIAL STATEMENT.
NO!! OUR OFFICIAL POSITION IS THAT THERE WAS NO FLOOD.
BUT IT'S ALL OVER THE NEWS CHANNELS!
NOPE! EGYPT NEVER GETS RAIN. ONLY DROUGHTS.
SIR, THE EGYPTIAN PEOPLE WON'T BELIEVE OUR LIES!
I DON'T CARE! AS LONG AS THE ETHIOPIAN GOVERNMENT DOES!
© 2010. Tarek Shahin. www.alkhancomics.com

Notes by the author:

* Countries in Africa have quarrelled about the right to the Nile River as a resource.

26 January 2010

NADA, I DON'T THINK I'LL EVER START A FAMILY.
I'M STILL REPULSED BY MEN EVER SINCE I WAS SEXUALLY ASSAULTED LAST YEAR.

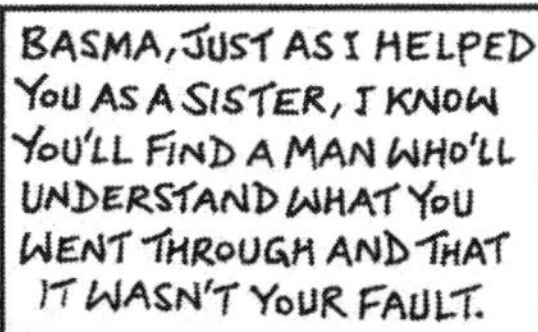
BASMA, JUST AS I HELPED YOU AS A SISTER, I KNOW YOU'LL FIND A MAN WHO'LL UNDERSTAND WHAT YOU WENT THROUGH AND THAT IT WASN'T YOUR FAULT.

YOU'RE SAYING I CAN FIND AN OPEN-MINDED MAN?
THINK POSITIVE!

HERE IN EGYPT?
THINK GLOBAL!

27 January 2010*

NADA, POLICE DAY WAS DECLARED AN EGYPTIAN NATIONAL HOLIDAY.
WHY'D YOU MAKE US COME TO WORK?

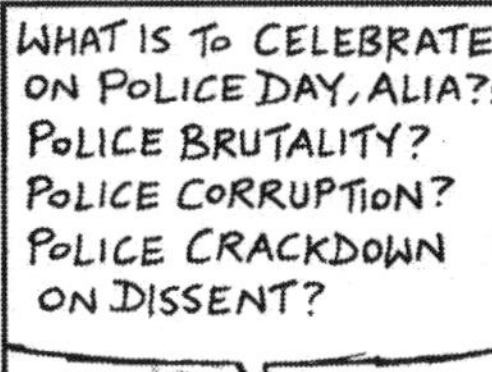
WHAT IS TO CELEBRATE ON POLICE DAY, ALIA?! POLICE BRUTALITY? POLICE CORRUPTION? POLICE CRACKDOWN ON DISSENT?

YOU'RE RIGHT. THEY ONLY PROTECT AND SERVE THE REGIME!
WE LIVE IN A POLICE STATE RUN BY THUGS!
IT MAKES ME SICK!!
NADA! ARE YOU ALRIGHT? YOU NEED TO CALM DOWN!
YES, I NEED A HOLIDAY! WHEN'S THE NEXT POLICE DAY?

30 January 2010

SO YOU MUST BE EBAA, MY FATHER'S SECOND WIFE.
OH, YOU'RE AISHA'S SON? THINK OF ME AS YOUR SECOND MOTHER!

BUT MY MOTHER IS BEAUTIFUL!
THE IMPORTANT THING IS A PERSON'S INNER BEAUTY!

MY MOTHER IS BEAUTIFUL ON THE OUTSIDE AND THE INSIDE.
WELL, MAYBE SOON I'LL HAVE CHILDREN OF MY OWN!

WELL, DON'T BE SCARED! THE IMPORTANT THING IS YOUR CHILDREN'S INNER BEAUTY.

Notes by the author:

* Exactly one year later the Egyptian uprising would begin on Police Day 2011.

1 February 2010

"DEAR HASSAN,
MY NAME IS OMAR SHUKRI AND I UNDERSTAND YOU ARE RUNNING AGAINST MY UNCLE IN THIS YEAR'S PARLIAMENTARY ELECTIONS, AND I WANT YOU TO KNOW...

"...ELECTIONS, AND I WANT YOU TO KNOW THAT I WILL DO MY BEST TO HELP MY UNCLE DEFEAT YOU, HASSAN. THE MUSLIM BROTHERHOOD CANNOT RULE EGYPT. ...

"I WILL NOT HELP YOU OR ANY OTHER MEMBER OF THE MUSLIM BROTHERHOOD TO DESTROY OUR BASIC CIVIL LIBERTIES."

WHAT IS THIS?! HEY, GUARD! I THOUGHT YOU SAID THIS WAS A LETTER FROM MY LAWYER!

NO! I TOLD YOU, YOU CAN'T GET A LAWYER UNTIL WE CHARGE YOU WITH A CRIME!

2 February 2010

YES, OMAR. I REMEMBER MY COVER STORY FROM FIVE YEARS AGO.
IT WAS ABOUT FEMALE GENITAL MUTILATION IN RURAL EGYPT.

NADA, WHEN MY GRANFATHER REFUSED TO APOLOGIZE FOR THAT ARTICLE IT COST MY UNCLE THE ELECTION!
FEMALE GENITAL MUTILATION IS A SENSITIVE ISSUE HERE IN THE VILLAGE!!

IT IS AN ISSUE I CARE ABOUT DEEPLY! THOSE AFFECTED EXPERIENCE EXCRUTIATING PAIN, LOSE CONTROL OVER THEIR BODILY FUNCTIONS AND CAN NO LONGER HAVE A HAPPY MARRIAGE!

NADA, THAT'S VERY TRUE! I'M GLAD YOU UNDERSTAND HOW LOSING THE ELECTION AFFECTED MY UNCLE.

3 February 2010

SO WHICH SIDE OF THE MUSLIM BROTHERHOOD DO YOU REPRESENT?
THERE ARE NO SIDES, OMAR. WE'RE ONE GROUP.

COME ON, HASSAN! EVERYONE KNOWS THERE'S A RIFT WITHIN THE BROTHERHOOD BETWEEN THE REFORMISTS AND THE CONSERVATIVES!

THE REFORMISTS STAND FOR CONSERVATIVE VALUES.

SO WHAT DO THE CONSERVATIVES STAND FOR?
THEY MOSTLY SIT.

4 February 2010

UNCLE AMIN, YOU'RE NOT A MEMBER OF THE NDP. WHY DO YOU THINK YOU CAN WIN AN ELECTION?! THE NDP HAS RULED EGYPT FOR THREE DECADES!

MY CAMPAIGN MESSAGE SAYS THAT THE PEOPLE WILL HAVE MORE JOBS, BETTER HEALTHCARE AND IMPROVED INFRASTRUCTURE.

ISN'T THAT THE EXACT SAME MESSAGE OF THE RULING PARTY?
YES. IT IS. EXCEPT, MY MESSAGE IS MUCH MORE BELIEVABLE!

HOW SO?
I ADDED "WILL" BEFORE "HAVE."

6 February 2010

YOUR PRICE HAS SUDDENLY MULTIPLIED FIVE-FOLD. MOST HOUSEHOLDS CAN NO LONGER AFFORD BUTANE COOKING GAS.

HAS THE MONEY CHANGED YOU?
NO! DEEP INSIDE, I'M STILL THE SAME OLD ME!
BUTANE COOKING GAS
EGP8
EGP40

CORRUPTION AND EGYPT'S FAILED ENERGY POLICIES HAVE BEEN BLAMED FOR YOUR SHORTAGE. WOULD YOU STILL VOTE FOR THE RULING PARTY?
BUTANE COOKING GAS
EGP8
EGP40

DO YOU NOT THINK THAT SHAKING THINGS UP WILL BE BETTER?
LADY, DEEP INSIDE, I'M ALL GAS! STABILITY WILL BE SAFER.
BUTANE COOKING GAS
EGP8
EGP40

10 February 2010

DR. EBAA'S JOURNAL ENTRY:
MY MARRIAGE TO DR. ANWAR IS HELPING MY RESEARCH ON POLYGAMY. I'M NOW ASSESSING WHY HIS FIRST WIFE FEELS SUFFOCATED BY...

UH... ANWAR! HI! MAY I PLEASE HAVE SOME PRIVACY?
WHY, EBAA? WHAT'S GOING ON?!

NOTHING! CAN'T A WOMAN HAVE SOME PRIVACY?!
YOUR MARRIAGE IS YOUR PRIVACY!

I THINK I DISAGREE!
WOMAN! KEEP YOUR THOUGHTS PRIVATE!

11 February 2010

WHAT?!! ANWAR, YOU ACTUALLY EXPECT ME TO COOK FOR YOU?!
AISHA DOES! DUTIES MUST BE SHARED BETWEEN WIVES.
I'M AN EDUCATED WOMAN! I DON'T COOK LIKE SOME SLAVE!
EBAA!! DON'T CALL AISHA A SLAVE!
IF YOU CARE ABOUT HER FEELINGS, WHY'D YOU MARRY ME?
I CAN LOVE YOU BOTH!
I DON'T BELIEVE YOU CAN!
HAVE FAITH. DON'T ASSUME YOU'RE A BAD COOK.

12 February 2010

OMAR WANTS HIS UNCLE TO REGAIN HIS POPULARITY AMONG HIS PEOPLE. HE'LL INSIST YOU APOLOGIZE FOR YOUR ARTICLE ON FEMALE CIRCUMCISION.
BIG FALAFEL, I'M SURRISED PEOPLE IN THE RURAL AREAS EVEN READ MY ARTICLE! I THOUGHT ILLITERACY WAS WIDESPREAD!
NADA, THEY DON'T HAVE TO READ IT! WHEN YOU BREAK SOCIAL TABOOS, ANGRY PEOPLE CAN SMELL IT!
HOW CAN THEY SMELL PRINTED WORDS?!
USING A BOX OF MATCHES.

15 February 2010

YOU SAY YOUR UNCLE IS RUNNING AGAINST HASSAN? HE'S CHALLENGING THE MUSLIM BROTHERHOOD?! YOUR UNCLE MUST BE A GREAT MAN!
THANK YOU, SIR.
العدل
SO YOU'RE TRYING TO CONVINCE HASSAN THAT THE MUSLIM BROTHERHOOD SHOULD NOT RUN IN THE ELECTIONS?
YES! BUT YOU KEEP INTERRUPTING OUR CONVERSATION BY ARRESTING HIM!
العدل
I'LL RELEASE HASSAN AT ONCE! BY THE WAY, YOUR UNCLE IS A GREAT MAN!!
YES. HE IS. HE'S RUNNING AS AN INDEPENDENT.
العدل
ANYWAY, HASSAN, SO AS I WAS SAYING...

16 February 2010

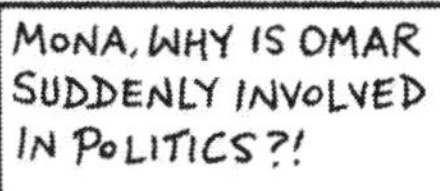
MONA, WHY IS OMAR SUDDENLY INVOLVED IN POLITICS?!

SOHA, HE REALLY WANTS HIS UNCLE TO WIN THE PARLIAMENTARY ELECTIONS.

WELL, HE'S MY NEPHEW TOO! AND I'D LIKE TO SEE THAT YOUNG MAN FINALLY GET MARRIED TO A NICE GIRL!

OUR ELECTIONS ARE FAKE AND AN INSULT TO THE INTELLI-GENCE!
UNFORTU-NATELY, THAT'S OMAR'S VIEW ON EGYPTIAN GIRLS!

17 February 2010

YOUR EXCELLENCY, THIS WEEK MOHAMED EL BARADEI WILL RETURN HOME TO CAIRO. MANY PEOPLE ARE EXPECTED TO GREET HIM AS THE NEW 'CONSENSUS PRESIDENT.'

HOW CAN THE MINISTRY OF PROSPERITY PREVENT THIS?
I SUGGEST WE MOVE THE AIRPORT OUT OF SIGHT!

THAT'S NOT HUMANLY POSSIBLE!
IT'S EITHER THAT OR MOVE PUBLIC OPINION!

CAIRO INTERNATIONAL AIRPORT
ARRIVALS
PUSH, YOUR EXCELLENCY! PUSH!

19 February 2010

FORMER IAEA CHIEF MOHAMED ELBARADEI RETURNS TO CAIRO AMID CHEERING SUPPORTERS.
WHY DID YOU COME HERE TO GREET HIM?
NOBLE NOBEL

BEFORE, I USED TO COME GREET THE NATIONAL FOOTBALL PLAYERS!! TODAY'S MY CHANCE TO MEET SOMEONE WHO ACTUALLY MATTERS!
WELCOME HOME
NOBLE NOBEL

ELBARADEI HAS MY VOTE. HE'S A GLOBALLY RECOG-NIZED THINKER WHO KNOWS THE INTERNATIONAL ARENA. HE'S MADE EGYPT PROUD. HE'S THE BEST ONE TO LEAD.
WELCOME HOME
NOBLE NOBEL
WHAT CAN ELBARADEI DO FOR EGYPT THAT THE CURRENT REGIME CAN'T?
HOPEFULLY, GET US INTO THE WORLD CUP.

20 February 2010

WOW, YUNAN! GREAT PHOTOS OF DR. MOHAMED ELBARADEI'S SUPPORTERS!
THEY HAVE SO MUCH HOPE THAT HIS PRESIDENTIAL CREDENTIALS WILL OVERCOME EGYPT'S FLAWED ELECTION SYSTEM!
ARE THOSE MORE PICTURES OF ELBARADEI'S SUPPORTERS?
NO. THESE ARE BYSTANDERS WHO DON'T HAVE HOPE.
THIS IS JUST A PICTURE OF ELBARADEI.

22 February 2010

INDEED, AS A EUROPEAN OFFICIAL I CAN SAY WE'RE OUTRAGED THAT THE AGENTS WHO ALLEGEDLY KILLED A HAMAS LEADER USED FAKE EUROPEAN PASSPORTS!! ISRAEL MUST GIVE ANSWERS.
SO YOU'RE ANGRY THAT THEY WERE ON FAKE PASSPORTS BUT OTHERWISE YOU'RE O.K. WITH POLITICAL ASSASSINATION?
UH... ISRAEL HAS A RIGHT TO DEFEND ITSELF BUT WE SUPPORT CIVILITY.
I THINK YOU'RE TIP-TOEING AROUND THE SUBJECT LIKE A COWARD!
WELL, I THINK YOU'RE VERY RUDE!
DON'T WORRY! I WASN'T BEING RUDE ON A FAKE PASSPORT!

24 February 2010

NO, OMAR! OF COURSE YOU CAN'T BORROW MY DONKEY FOR A WHOLE YEAR! IN A YEAR'S TIME IT'LL BE A YEAR OLDER!
ALRIGHT, HASSAN. HOW ABOUT WHEN I RETURN YOUR DONKEY IN A YEAR'S TIME, I COMPENSATE YOU FOR ITS LOST VALUE BY GIVING YOU A FRUIT BASKET?
VERY FUNNY, OMAR! IS THAT YOUR LAME WAY OF ARGUING TO THE MUSLIM BROTHERHOOD THAT INTEREST RATES ARE NOT USURY?!
WE NEED A STRONGER METAPHOR THAN A FRUIT BASKET!
YOU MEAN A HIGHER INTEREST RATE?

27 February 2010

MAMA! SO YOU'RE DANCING AT PRIVATE PARTIES NOW?
NO, NADA! THIS IS A PUBLIC GATHERING!
You are cordially invited to celebrate the union of Egypt's Secular Opposition and The Muslim Brotherhood
OH, COME ON!! EVEN A BLIND PERSON CAN SEE THROUGH THIS!
YOU MEAN MY DANCE OUTFIT? I'M JUST FOLLOWING THE DRESS CODE!
Dress Code: Maximum Appeal

2 March 2010

DR. EBAA, YOU FOOLED ANWAR INTO MARRYING YOU AND IN THE PROCESS YOU CRUSHED AISHA, HIS FIRST WIFE! AND NOW YOU'RE BEGGING FOR MY HELP?!
I DID IT FOR RESEARCH! TO BETTER ADDRESS WOMEN'S ISSUES! BUT NOW MY LIFE IS UNBEARABLE! ANWAR TREATS ME LIKE A SLAVE! I CAN'T DEAL WITH THIS ON MY OWN!
YOUR INTENTIONS WERE GOOD. BUT YOUR METHODS MADE IT WORSE FOR AISHA!
YOU'RE RIGHT, NADA. I DESERVE TO HANDLE THIS BURDEN ALONE!
NO. YOU DON'T. I'LL FIND A WAY TO HELP YOU.
GREAT! SO YOU'RE WILLING TO JOIN AS A THIRD WIFE?

3 March 2010

NADA'S COVER STORY ON FEMALE GENITAL MUTILATION WAS SPOT ON! EGYPT HAS ONE OF THE HIGHEST RATES OF FGM IN THE WORLD!
I KNOW, ALIA! BUT THERE ARE SO MANY OTHER PROBLEMS IN EGYPT WE COULD'VE WRITTEN ABOUT! SO LET'S BRAINSTORM SOME TOPICS!!
I CAN'T THINK OF MANY THAT ARE MORE IMPORTANT THAN FGM!
OK, SO 'LIMITED THINKING.' THAT'S A GOOD TOPIC, ALIA.
NO, OMAR! I MEAN IF I HAD TO CHOOSE I'D PICK FGM!
AH! ANOTHER GOOD ONE. 'THE ILLUSION OF CHOICE.' KEEP 'EM COMING, ALIA!

4 March 2010

PLEASE, HAJJA FOLLA! YOU CAN'T KICK ME OUT OF MY HOME!
I OWN THE BUILDING, MR. LEVY. AND YOU HAVEN'T PAID THE RENT!
PLEASE BE PATIENT! I'M ONLY HERE AS A STUDENT!
MIDDLE EAST STUDIES, RIGHT?
WHAT IS IT WITH YOU WESTERNERS ALWAYS STUDYING IN CAIRO?
I'M IN A SPECIAL PROGRAMME FOR THE YOUTH.
A S.P.Y.?
WE DON'T CALL IT THAT!
© 2010. Tarek Shahin. www.alkhancomics.com

5 March 2010

OMAR, WHY ARE YOU SO WOR.....
YUNAN! AS A COPT YOU SHOULD BE EVEN MORE WORRIED THAN I AM!
YOU THINK IF THE MUSLIM BROTHERHOOD RULE, COPTIC CHRISTIANS WILL HAVE ANY CIVIL RIGHTS?!
FIRST I NEED TO HEAR THEIR POLI.....
THEIR SLOGAN IS "ISLAM IS THE SOLUTION!"
OMAR!!! CAN I GET A CHANCE TO SPEAK?!
I HIGHLY DOUBT IT.
© 2010. Tarek Shahin. www.alkhancomics.com

6 March 2010

BROTHER LEVY, YOU WERE EVICTED BECAUSE YOU CAN'T AFFORD THE RENT?! THEN YOU MUST COME STAY WITH ME!!
WHAT? ANWAR, THAT'S THE NICEST THING ANYONE HAS EVER DONE FOR ME... BUT WHAT ABOUT YOUR WIVES?
THAT IS WHAT FACE VEILS ARE FOR.
OH, THAT'S RIGHT. YOUR WIVES BOTH WEAR THE NIQAB.
AND THE BATHROOM IS THREE STEPS FORWARD, TWO STEPS RIGHT.
© 2010. Tarek Shahin. www.alkhancomics.com

8 March 2010

I WILL NOT APOLOGIZE FOR AN ARTICLE JUST SO YOUR FAMILY CAN WIN THE VILLAGE ELECTIONS!
OMAR, I THOUGHT YOU WERE A LIBERAL!!

WOULD YOU RATHER THE MUSLIM BROTHERHOOD WIN?!
NADA, IF THEY RULE EGYPT IT WILL BE A CATASTROPHE FOR BOTH ME AND YOU!!

FOR ME BECAUSE EGYPT'S PEACE WITH ISRAEL IS ESSENTIAL FOR FOREIGN PRIVATE INVESTMENT!
FOR YOU BECAUSE THE MUSLIM BROTHERS WERE THE ENEMY OF YOUR BELOVED HERO NASSER!!

DO YOU UNDERS-TAND?!
WHY NASSER AND THE MUSLIM BROTHERS DIDN'T GET ALONG?
GOOD QUESTION!

9 March 2010

ANWAR DIDN'T BELIEVE ME WHEN I TOLD HIM YOU ONLY MARRIED HIM FOR RESEARCH.
SO WHAT MAKES YOU THINK HE'LL DIVORCE ME?!

HE CAN TELL YOU DON'T LOVE HIM BECAUSE YOU DON'T OBEY HIM!
DR. EBAA, DID YOU REALLY THINK YOU COULD KEEP UP THE ACT?!!

AISHA, WHAT I DID HURT YOU, BUT BELIEVE ME, IT WAS AGAINST MY NATURE AND HURT MY CONSCIENCE EVEN MORE.
CAN YOU AND I BE FRIENDS?

FRIENDS?! YOU JUST ADMITTED TO VICIOUSLY STEALING MY HUSBAND!!
YES. YOUR TURN TO TELL ME SOMETHING ABOUT YOURSELF!

10 March 2010

GOD SAVE US!!! ANWAR! I JUST MADE TWO DISCOVERIES ABOUT YOUR SECOND WIFE!
IS EBAA ALRIGHT?

EBAA IS PREGNANT.
REALLY? LISTEN, AISHA. THIS DOES NOT MEAN I'LL LOVE HER MORE THAN YOU.

WAIT! AND SHE'S ONE OF THOSE!
WHAT ARE YOU TRYING TO SAY?

SHE'S ATTRACTED TO WOMEN!
SO AM I! WHAT ARE YOU TRYING TO SAY?

11 March 2010

I WAS BORN THIS WAY. IT'S WHY I LEFT EGYPT WHEN I WAS YOUNG.
ANWAR, OUR FARCICAL MARRIAGE WAS TORTURE!
I COULDN'T HELP BUT MAKE A PASS AT AISHA!

EBAA, YOU'RE A HOMOSEXUAL?!!!
YOU KNOW WHAT THIS MEANS?!
WE'LL ALL BE WIPED OUT ANY SECOND NOW!!
AISHA, LET'S HIDE!!

PLEASE FORGIVE US! PLEASE FORGIVE US!

ANWAR, MAYBE THE EDITOR WON'T CENSOR THE COMIC STRIP!
SHE WILL! ANY SECOND NOW!! PLEASE FORGIVE US!

12 March 2010

NADA, MY MARRIAGE TO ANWAR STARTED AS A RESEARCH PROJECT. BUT HE'S SO FERTILE! AND GAY ADOPTION LAWS IN THE STATES KEEP CHANGING!

I REALLY WANTED A BABY OF MY OWN!
TO THINK THIS ALL STARTED BECAUSE I WROTE A BAD REVIEW OF YOUR BOOK!

DR. EBAA, ANWAR WILL TRY TO FORCEFULLY TAKE YOUR BABY! HE WON'T LET HIS CHILD BE RAISED ABROAD BY A LESBIAN!

NO! HE CAN'T STEAL MY BABY! I WANT MY CHILD TO HAVE MY WRITING STYLE!
THIS ISN'T THE BEST WAY TO WIN MY SUPPORT.

15 March 2010

EBAA, I'M APPALLED TO DISCOVER THAT YOU ARE A LESBIAN.
YOUR HOMOSEXUALITY IS IN DEFIANCE OF ISLAM!

BUT, STILL, I'M CURIOUS! HOW DO YOU AND YOUR FEMALE LOVER ACTUALLY, PHYSICALLY....?
I MEAN WHO IS THE.... AND WHO IS THE....?

I MEAN, WHICH ONE OF YOU IS THE....?
ANWAR, JUST SAY IT!!

WHEN YOU'RE BOTH PRAYING, WHICH ONE OF YOU STANDS IN FRONT?

16 March 2010

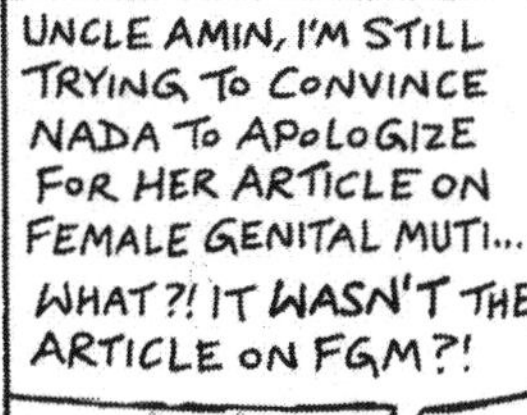

UNCLE AMIN, I'M STILL TRYING TO CONVINCE NADA TO APOLOGIZE FOR HER ARTICLE ON FEMALE GENITAL MUTI.... WHAT?! IT WASN'T THE ARTICLE ON FGM?!

ENVY?! SHE WROTE AN EDITORIAL DESCRIBING EGYPT'S OBSESSION WITH ENVY AS SUPERSTITION? AND THAT'S WHAT ANGERED THE VILLAGERS?

AND YOU BLAME THAT EDITORIAL ABOUT ENVY FOR YOUR LOSING THE VILLAGE ELECTIONS?
OH! YOU BLAME THAT EDITORIAL ABOUT ENVY AND YOU BLAME PEOPLE'S ENVY?

18 March 2010

YOU MIGHT SIDE WITH OMAR? YOU WANT NADA TO APOLOGIZE FOR HER 'TABOO' WRITINGS? YUNAN, WHAT HAPPENED TO THE JOURNALIST I FELL IN LOVE WITH?!

MARIAN, WHAT HAPPENED IS WE'RE NOW EXPECTING!! I DON'T WANT OUR COPTIC CHILD TO GROW UP IN AN EGYPT POSSIBLY RULED BY THE MUSLIM BROTHERHOOD!

YUNAN, EVER SINCE I GOT PREGNANT YOU'VE BEEN CONSUMED BY FEAR! YOU FEAR OUR INCOME WON'T BE HIGH ENOUGH, EGYPT WON'T BE FREE ENOUGH, THE WORLD WON'T BE BIG ENOUGH!

IS THERE NO PLACE THAT YOU THINK WILL BE SAFE FOR OUR CHILD?!
HOW LONG CAN YOU KEEP IT IN YOUR TUMMY?

19 March 2010

HOLD ON! MY FRIEND ANWAR'S SECOND WIFE IS DR. EBAA ANTAR? THE SELF-EXILED EGYPTIAN-AMERICAN SOCIOLOGIST? HOW?!!

I SUGGESTED SHE STUDY POLYGAMY. SHE WENT TOO FAR!
NO, NADA. I MEAN HOW IS IT THAT SHE'S GAY?!

OMAR, SOME WOMEN HAVE THAT SEXUAL INSTINCT.
I KNOW. BUT HOW COULD ANWAR NOT TELL THAT SHE WAS FAKING IT?!

SADLY, MOST WOMEN HAVE THAT SURVIVAL INSTINCT.

22 March 2010

SO YOU'RE NADA, THE JOURNALIST WHO INTERVENED IN MY HOME!
YOU MUST BE DR. ANWAR, THE POLYGAMIST.
WATCH YOUR MOUTH, WOMAN!
ANWAR! NO! TAKE IT BACK! FEAR NADA'S WRATH!
OMAR, I ONLY FEAR GOD'S WRATH.
NO! NO! I'VE SEEN GOD'S WRATH!
GOD FORGIVES!

23 March 2010

AISHA, ANWAR CAN'T KEEP DR. EBAA PRISONER WHILE SHE DELIVERS HIS BABY!
HER SEXUAL ORIENTATION DOESN'T MEAN IT'S NOT HER BABY TOO!

MS. NADA, I TOLD ANWAR TO BE CIVIL AND RELEASE EBAA!
SO WHY MUST YOU WRITE A NEWS STORY ABOUT THIS?! STOP MEDDLING IN OUR PRIVATE AFFAIRS!!

I MUST SHED LIGHT ON A MESS LIKE THIS.
IT'S A JOURNALIST THING. YOU WOULDN'T UNDERSTAND.

SHEDDING LIGHT ON A MESS MAKES IT BIGGER.
IT'S A HOMEMAKER THING. YOU WOULDN'T UNDERSTAND.

24 March 2010

WITH YOUR HELP, OMAR, I'LL WIN A SEAT ON PARLIAMENT, AND THEN I MAY FINALLY GET A BUILDING PERMIT ON MY FARM LAND!

A BUILDING PERMIT?!!! THAT'S THE ONLY REASON YOU'RE RUNNING FOR PARLIAMENT?!
UNCLE AMIN, I THOUGHT YOU WERE RUNNING AS AN INDEPENDENT TO HELP FIGHT CORRUPTION!!

I'M BUILDING A HOSPITAL FOR THE VILLAGERS! IT'LL MEAN DOUBLE THE HEALTH CARE, DOUBLE THE EMPLOYMENT OPPORTUNITIES, DOUBLE THE SOCIAL BENEFIT!

DOUBLE THE RETURN ON YOUR INVESTMENT?

25 March 2010

A MISCARRIAGE? OH MY GOD, MARIAN!
IT JUST.... HAPPENED.
AND YUNAN DOESN'T KNOW YET?
I COULDN'T TELL HIM. IT'S WHY I CALLED YOU, ALIA.
SOMEHOW YOU KNOW HOW TO BREAK BAD NEWS TO YUNAN! LIKE BACK WHEN YOU TOLD HIM HE DIDN'T WIN PHOTOGRAPHER OF THE YEAR!
HE HANDLED IT WELL WHEN THE NEWS CAME FROM YOU.
IT ALSO HELPED THAT HE WON PHOTO-GRAPHER OF THE DECADE!
© 2010. Tarek Shahin. www.alkhancomics.com

26 March 2010

SO WHAT IF YOU HAD A MISCARRIAGE? WE'LL TRY AGAIN. I PROMISE FROM HERE ON I'LL NEVER BE AFRAID OF THE FUTURE! I LOVE YOU, MARIAN.
NOT JUST YUNAN. ME TOO. YOU'RE HIS WIFE, WHICH MAKES YOU MY DAUGHTER. AS FOR YOUR MOTHER-IN-LAW, YOU KNOW YOU'RE ALWAYS IN HER THOUGHTS.
GOD, WHY?! IF YOU HAD TO TAKE SOMEONE WHY COULDN'T YOU HAVE TAKEN HER INSTEAD OF MY GRANDCHILD? GOD, WHY?!
CONGRATULATIONS, MARIAN. YOU'RE NOW ALSO IN HER PRAYERS!
© 2010. Tarek Shahin. www.alkhancomics.com

27 March 2010

MARIAN, YOU'RE YUNAN'S WIFE. I LOVE YOU AS A DAUGHTER.
I WAS JUST BEING A SILLY MOTHER-IN-LAW. I APOLOGIZE FOR ALL THE NASTY THINGS I'VE SAID. I'M TRULY SORRY.
AND YOUR FATHER-IN-LAW TOO! HE'S ALSO SORRY.
ME?! I'VE ONLY SAID NICE THINGS ABOUT MARIAN!
I HEARD YOU TELL OUR SON, "LOVE HER BECAUSE YOU'RE STUCK WITH HER."
I WAS REFE-RRING TO YOU!!
© 2010. Tarek Shahin. www.alkhancomics.com

29 March 2010

EGYPT'S PRESIDENT, 81, RETURNS TO CAIRO THREE WEEKS AFTER SURGERY IN A GERMAN HOSPITAL.
WHERE WERE YOU WHEN YOU HEARD THE PRESIDENT WAS BACK?
I WAS STANDING IN LINE TO GET BREAD.
I HAVE NOTHING AGAINST THE PRESIDENT PERSONALLY. ALL I WANT IS INSTANT CHANGE. BUT I DON'T WISH HIM BAD HEALTH.
CAN YOU HAVE ONE WITHOUT THE OTHER?
BREAD WITHOUT LINES? NOT WITHOUT CHANGE.

30 March 2010

NADA, NOT ONLY WILL WE NOT APOLOGIZE FOR YOUR PREVIOUS ARTICLES, WE'LL ALSO RUN THE STORY ON DR. EBAA'S CAPTIVITY.
YES !!! OMAR, YOU REALIZE BOTH YOUR UNCLE AND YOUR FRIEND ANWAR WILL SEVER TIES WITH YOU FOREVER! AREN'T YOU SCARED?
YUNAN THOUGHT THE FUTURE WAS TOO SCARY FOR HIS CHILD, AND THEN HE LOST HIS BABY IN A SPLIT SECOND! I SAY NOTHING IS SCARY ANYMORE.
YOU AND I ARE FINALLY ON THE SAME PAGE! HOW DOES IT FEEL?
FEELS GOOD. SCARY, BUT GOOD.

31 March 2010

GIRLS, I REALIZE NOW THAT MY FILM AUDIENCES HAVE BEEN LAUGHING AT ME, NOT WITH ME! I SACRIFICED ART FOR COMMERCIAL APPEAL!
NAHED HABIB
CREAMY SEWAGE
I GOT SO GREEDY THAT I LEFT YOUR FATHER, AN INTELLIGENT PLAYWRIGHT WHO REFUSED TO PROFIT FROM THE DEMISE OF EGYPTIAN CULTURE!
HE WAS A GREAT MAN. A GREAT LOVER! NADA, WILL YOUR FATHER EVER TAKE ME BACK?
I'LL THINK ABOUT IT.

1 April 2010

OMAR'S PETTY MAGAZINE ACTUALLY WROTE ABOUT ME AND EBAA!
IT SAYS YOU'RE STOPPING YOUR WIFE FROM FLYING TO AMERICA!
ALKHAN NEWS
YOUR WIFE EXPLOITS YOUR HOME AND TRIES TO STEAL YOUR BABY AND NOW THE WORLD THINKS YOU ARE THE VILLAIN FOR RESTRICTING HER FREEDOM?
ALKHAN!
SEE, BROTHER LEVY? NO ONE IN THE ENTIRE WORLD WILL HEAR MY SIDE OF THE STORY!
WHY? BECAUSE I'M THE BIG, BAD ARAB MAN!
BROTHER LEVY, WILL YOU HEAR THE STORY OF THE ARAB MAN?
SURE, BROTHER ANWAR! I'M NOT EXACTLY AN ANTI-SEMITE.
© 2010. Tarek Shahin. www.alkhancomics.com

3 April 2010

HASSAN, I FEAR THE MUSLIM BROTHERS' "ISLAM IS THE SOLUTION" POLICY IS NOT THE ANSWER FOR EGYPT.
BUT I WON'T USE MY MEDIA POWER TO FIGHT YOU.
LET'S HOPE DEMOCRACY CAN RUN ITS COURSE.
THAT'S WHAT I PRAY FOR, OMAR.
MAY THE BEST MAN WIN, HASSAN!
MAY THE BEST MAN WIN, OMAR!
LISTEN, WOULD YOU PLEASE ALSO PRAY THAT WHEN THE BEST MAN WINS, HE, TOO, WILL BAN YOU?
© 2010. Tarek Shahin. www.alkhancomics.com

6 April 2010

NADA, MY FRIEND ANWAR IS ANGRY YOU WROTE ABOUT HIM.
GOOD! HE'S CRUEL TO HIS WIVES! HE'S A TYRANT!
ARE YOU OFFICIALLY CONCERNED ABOUT BOTH HIS WIVES?
WELL, HIS WIFE EBAA IS A U.S. CITIZEN. HER SAFETY IS OUR PRIORITY.
WHAT'S THAT ON TV?
THE WHITE HOUSE WILL NOT LET THIS DR. ANWAR KEEP HIS WIFE EBAA AT HIS HOME IN EGYPT.
HE IS CRUEL TO HIS WIVES AND CLEARLY A TYRANT.
NADA?
Anwar is the Best.
F K the West.
© 2010. Tarek Shahin. www.alkhancomics.com

7 April 2010

NADA, FIRST YOU CALL MY FRIEND ANWAR A CRUEL HUSBAND AND NOW YOU ARE SUPPORTING HIM JUST BECAUSE THE WEST SHARES YOUR VIEW?!
ANWAR IS the Best
IF ANWAR'S WIFE WASN'T A U.S. CITIZEN, AMERICA WOULDN'T GIVE A SHIT!
I AGREE! BUT WHY DOES THAT CHANGE YOUR CORE VIEW?
BECAUSE, OMAR, IT'S FOREIGN INTERVENTION IN A DOMESTIC MATTER!
I AGREE! BUT WHY DOES THAT CHANGE YOUR CORE VIEW?
OMAR, YOU'RE BACK ON MY SIDE? BUT YOU CALLED ME A CROOK!
YOU FIND THIS HARD TO UNDERSTAND? TRY ARABISM!
AL KHAN SORRY FOR ALL WRITINGS OF NADA
UNCLE AMIN FOR PARLI-AMENT

8 April 2010

I AM EGYPT'S MINISTER OF PROSPERITY! I AM CLEARLY NOT DOING MY JOB IF THERE'S A NATIONWIDE HASHISH SHORTAGE!!
أزمة الحشيش
SIR, THERE'S NO HASHISH SHORTAGE! WE JUST HAD TO REDIRECT SUPPLIES TO THE PRO-DEMOCRACY PROTESTS!! THEY WERE GETTING EXCESSIVELY VIOLENT!
SO YOU'RE USING THE HASHISH TO CALM VIOLENT PROTESTERS?
NOT THE PROTE-STERS.
LIKE, DON'T... PROTEST, MAAAN!
TIME FOR CHANGE

9 April 2010

MY NECK HURTS, MY BACK HURTS, MY TOES HURT! DR. ANWAR, YOU MUST FIX THIS! AFTER ALL, IT IS YOUR FAULT I FELL ILL!
EVER SINCE YOU DISCOVERED THAT YOUR SECOND WIFE IS A HEATHEN HOMOSEXUAL, GOD HAS MADE EVERYONE IN OUR NEIGHBORHOOD SICK! AS PUNISHMENT!
I KNOW, AND I'M SORRY! I'LL OFFER YOU FREE TREATMENT.
I NEED SOMETHING STRONGER.
I TOLD YOU, I WILL NOT SLAY MY WIFE!!
AND YOU CALL YOURSELF A DOCTOR?!

10 April 2010

PREVIOUSLY ON 'AL KHAN'...
BROTHER LEVY, IF YOU CAN'T AFFORD THE RENT, YOU CAN COME STAY AT OUR HOME!
REALLY? THANKS, ANWAR!

MAYBE WE SHOULDN'T DO THIS! ALLAH MIGHT PUNISH US!
DR. ANWAR SHOULD'VE KILLED HIS WIFE WHEN HE FOUND OUT SHE WAS GAY!!

THERE SHE IS. SLEEPING UNDER THE COVERS!
WELL, HURRY! BEFORE DR. ANWAR COMES HOME!

DIE, YOU HEATHEN LESBIAN!
BROTHER ANWAR?

12 April 2010

YOU TRIED TO KILL A GAY INFIDEL?! THAT IS SO 1990s!
BESIDES, I THOUGHT WE HAD A DEAL!

WE'D ARREST GAYS AND ATHEISTS AND IN RETURN YOU EXTREMISTS WOULD STOP VIOLENTLY IMPLEMENTING YOUR INTERPRETATION OF SHARIA!

BUT WHAT YOU DID THIS MORNING HAS GIVEN US AN EXCUSE TO INITIATE A NEW CRACKDOWN ON ANYONE WITH A BEARD!!

YOUR TORTURE METHODS WILL CREATE MORE TERRORISTS!
NO, TRUST ME, WE CREATE MORE GAYS!

13 April 2010

YES, SIR, THE CULPRIT WAS SOME EXTREMIST WHO WANTED TO KILL A GAY AMERICAN WRITER BUT KILLED A JEWISH BRITISH EXPAT BY MISTAKE.

NO, SIR, IT WAS AN ISOLATED INCIDENT. YEAH, THE CULPRIT IS BEARDED BUT HE HAS NO AFFILIATION WITH THE MUSLIM BROTHERHOOD.

WHAT? SIR, I KNOW WE HAVE ELECTIONS SOON, BUT WE CAN'T TELL THE WHITE HOUSE THAT THE CULPRIT IS WITH THE MUSLIM BROTHERHOOD! IT'S WRONG TO LIE!!

FAX
FROM: EGYPTIAN MINISTRY OF PROSPERITY
RE: DEAD JEW
KILLER BEARDED. GUESS WHO?
-REGARDS.

14 April 2010

MY BEST FRIEND DIED IN MY OWN HOME! POOR BROTHER LEVY! HE WAS A GOOD MUSLIM.
NOAH LEVY WAS A GOOD GUY! LISTEN, ANWAR, NOAH WOULD HAVE WANTED ME TO TELL YOU THAT HE WAS OF THE JEWISH FAITH.
JEWISH?! OMAR, NO! LEVY WAS A FRIEND!
WHAT DOES THAT TELL US?
IT TELLS ME THAT LEVY WAS A GOOD MUSLIM!
NO, BROTHER. IT TELLS ME THAT YOU ARE.
© 2010. Tarek Shahin. www.alkhancomics.com

15 April 2010

WHAT?! BUT WE'RE HERE IN CAIRO TO COLLECT OUR SON'S BODY!
I TRIED TO TELL ANWAR THAT NOAH WAS JEWISH!
MR. AND MRS. LEVY, TO HONOR YOUR SON'S MEMORY, I COLLECTED DONATIONS TO BUILD 'THE BROTHER NOAH LEVY MOSQUE.'
OY VEY!! ARE YOU TELLING ME OUR SON NOAH IS BURIED UNDER THIS MOSQUE?
CAN WE KEEP IT?
© 2010. Tarek Shahin. www.alkhancomics.com

16 April 2010

SALEH, REMEMBER WHEN WE WERE YOUNG, WHY WE FELL IN LOVE?
WE WANTED TO USE ART TO CHANGE THE WORLD.
WELL, I'VE DECIDED TO USE WHAT'S LEFT OF MY FILM REVENUES TO BUILD SCHOOLS ACROSS EGYPT!
I HOPE WE'RE NOT TOO OLD TO TRY TO CHANGE THE WORLD!
NAHED, I SEE THE SAME YOUNG WOMAN I FELL IN LOVE WITH!
YOU'RE SWEET. CAN YOU TELL I'VE HAD SOME PLASTIC SURGERY?
SOME? I'M GLAD YOU HAVE ANY MONEY LEFT TO BUILD SCHOOLS!
© 2010. Tarek Shahin. www.alkhancomics.com

17 April 2010

DEMOCRACY FOR EGYPT

YES! I GOT ONE!
PLEASE, MAN! WE'RE JUST FOLLOWING ORDERS!
TIME FOR CHANGE

THINK HOW YOUR MOTHER WOULD FEEL IF SHE SAW YOU!
MY MOTHER NEVER TAUGHT ME HOW TO THINK!

BY "MOTHER" I MEANT EGYPT!
SO DID I.

19 April 2010

HELLO YUNAN. I'M OMAR'S MOTHER.
MADAM MONA! OF COURSE. PLEASE COME IN.

OMAR WAS GRIEVING, AND THEN YOUR WIFE HAD THE MISCARRIAGE. I DIDN'T KNOW WHEN TO PRESENT THE LAST WILL WRITTEN BY OMAR'S GRANDFATHER.

"I love Omar and I know he tried his best. But his conduct has proven that the business of journalism and the content of journalism can never be reconciled..."

"... And, so, I leave the ownership of Al Khan to photojournalist Yunan Salib. Yunan, it's your baby now, and it needs a diaper change."

20 April 2010

BUT I'M THE HEIR! HOW COULD MY GRAN-DFATHER LEAVE AL KHAN TO...
YES!! FINALLY, THE WORKERS WILL OWN THE ENTE-RPRISE!

OMAR, AS PUBLISHER YOU BLOCKED STORIES! AND NADA, AS EDITOR YOU COULD NEVER SEPARATE YOURSELF FROM THE NEWS YOU WERE REPORTING!

YOU WILL ALWAYS LET YOUR CONFLICTING IDEALS GET THE BETTER OF YOU. I LOVE YOU BOTH... BUT YOU'RE BOTH FIRED! THERE! I SAID IT!

YUNAN, STOP PRACTICING IN THE BATHROOM! COME SAY IT TO THEIR FACES!

21 April 2010

YUNAN IS RIGHT. I WAS A SCARED ACTIVIST HIDING INSIDE A BRAVE JOURNALIST!
I WAS HIDING MY INEFFECTIVENESS BEHIND MY "OBJECTIVITY."

FROM NOW ON, YOU FOCUS ON FIGHTING FOR THE ISSUES YOU CARE MOST ABOUT. AND I'LL FOCUS ON TELLING YOU THE NEWS!
THEN TELL ME, WILL THERE BE ANY GOOD NEWS FOR EGYPT? FOR THE PEOPLE? IS THERE HOPE?

I MEAN, WHAT HAPPENS NEXT?
THE FUTURE? NADA, YOU'RE THE ACTIVIST! YOU TELL ME!

22 April 2010

OVERWHELMED BY THE DEATH OF BROTHER LEVY, ANWAR LET ME RETURN TO THE STATES AND WE AGREED TO NEGOTIATE CHILD CUSTODY.
EBAA ANTAR, PhD
CORN FLAKES

MY POORLY RESEARCHED BOOKS ON EGYPT - MY BIRTHPLACE - ULTIMATELY DISTURBED ITS PEACE.
EBAA ANTAR, PhD

BUT NOW I CAN WRITE ABOUT MY EXPERIENCE! NOW THAT I'VE DONE MY RESEARCH, MY NEXT BOOK WILL NOT CAUSE ANY MORE PROBLEMS.
EBAA ANTAR, PhD

EGYPT
DR. EBAA ANTAR
MY STORY IN THE SOURCE OF THE NILE

23 April 2010

WOW, GRANDFATHER! DID I DO SUCH A BAD JOB RUNNING YOUR PUBLICATION THAT YOU HAD TO FIRE ME FROM BEYOND THE GRAVE?!

YOU KNOW WHAT? IT'S FINE! IT'S CAPITALISM! WHEN I WAS A BANKER IN LONDON I LEARNED ONE RULE: "DO IT RIGHT OR LEAVE."

I WON'T LEAVE CAIRO. SO I'LL FIND OTHER WAYS TO MAKE MY FAMILY PROUD.
IT'S TOO IMPORTANT TO ME!

...OR TO USE ANOTHER BANKING PHRASE:
I'M TOO BIG TO FAIL.

24 April 2010*

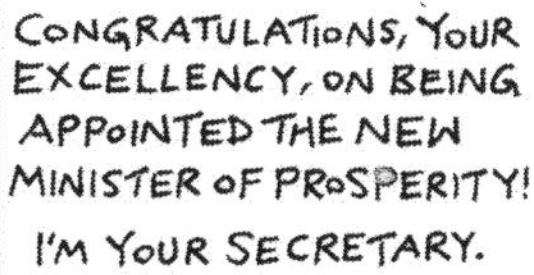
CONGRATULATIONS, YOUR EXCELLENCY, ON BEING APPOINTED THE NEW MINISTER OF PROSPERITY!
I'M YOUR SECRETARY.

SO WHY WAS MY PREDECESSOR REMOVED? PUBLIC PRESSURE? WAS HE A THREAT?
WHERE IS HE NOW?
CABINET RESHUFFLE: DR. AMGAD GAD MOVED!

AS MINISTER OF PROSPERITY, DR. GAD FAILED TO PLEASE EVERYONE. AS A RESULT, HE NOW HAS NO PUBLIC SUPPORT AND NO LOYAL FRIENDS.

I, AMGAD GAD, VOW TO HONOR MY NEW ROLE AS EGYPT'S FIRST VICE PRESIDENT IN 29 YEARS.

26 April 2010

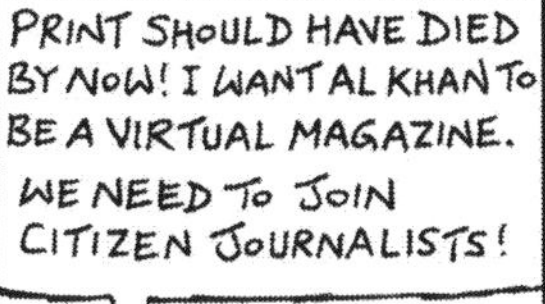
PRINT SHOULD HAVE DIED BY NOW! I WANT AL KHAN TO BE A VIRTUAL MAGAZINE.
WE NEED TO JOIN CITIZEN JOURNALISTS!

AL KHAN

YUNAN, IF AL KHAN EMBRACES ONLINE CITIZEN JOURNALISM, HOW WILL THE MAGAZINE MAKE MONEY?

ALIA, AS THE NEW EDITOR-IN-CHIEF IT'S NOT YOUR JOB TO WORRY ABOUT HOW WE MAKE MONEY!

THAT SAID, WE SHOULD FIND PAYING JOBS ON THE SIDE.

27 April 2010

CHANGE

CHANGE

Notes by the author:

* Mubarak's first concession after the uprising on 25 January 2011 was to appoint a VP.

28 April 2010

FIN
النهاية
MY THANKS TO ALL READERS

Notes by the author:

Despite its success and growing readership, I decided at that point to end this cartoon series because I was hoping against hope that the Egypt I was writing about was coming to an end and that a new one was about to rise.

Less than nine months after the end of the series, the Egyptian people took to Tahrir Square in peaceful protest. The glass ceiling of fear was broken. I was proud to be with them.
In Tahrir Square I saw Omar. I saw Nada. I saw Yunan. I saw Anwar.
I believe Big Falafel was there.

After eighteen days of protests, the authoritarian regime of Hosni Mubarak relinquished power on 11 February 2011. It's a start.

Thank you for reading.
Tarek Shahin

WHO WERE THEY SO ANGRY AT?
Change
تغيير

About the author

The Name
Tarek Shahin

The Birth
1982 in Cairo, Egypt

The Day
Asset management

The Night
Cartoons

The Contact
tarekshahin@gmail.com